Tom,

Thanks for all you do!

Jay Stockard
12/00

Mud River Tales

A COLLECTION OF STORIES IN RHYME

Mud River Tales

A COLLECTION OF STORIES IN RHYME

Lawrence Lyman Pauley

Written and Illustrated by
Lawrence Lyman Pauley

DiscoveryPress
WEST VIRGINIA

Library of Congress Catalog Card Number: 00-105887
ISBN: 0-9667246-2-3

First Edition, First Printing

Printed in Canada

Book and Cover Design: Mark S. Phillips

DiscoveryPress
945 Fourth Avenue, Suite 200A
Huntington, WV 25701
mdg@cloh.net

TABLE OF CONTENTS

DEDICATED

To the memory of my beloved grandfather,
Garfield Lyman Pauley,
whose example of character and integrity
has been my lifelong inspiration;
and to the memory of my dear brother,
Billy Wayne Pauley,
without whose leadership, courage and
spirit of adventure, many of the events
recounted in these tales may never have occurred.

PREFACE

This work, the ***Mud River Tales***, has been more than twenty years in the writing and a lifetime in the preparation. I did not set out to write a book. I have always loved poetry. So, as these stories emerged from my memory and it occurred to me that I should write them down and preserve them for my children, it seemed only natural to use the poetic form to express them. Friends and co-workers found them interesting and even entertaining and, as word got around, with increasing frequency, I was invited to present them orally, as a program, at meetings of various organizations. One question which has always come up at such meetings is, "Where can we obtain a book of your poems?" The ***Mud River Tales*** is the answer to that question.

The events reported in these tales actually occurred, and the participants in those events are real people. While striving to present these stories in an interesting and entertaining manner, I have endeavored to remain faithful to the facts, as I recall them. However, I must allow that there may be some, whose recollection of the events differs from my own. The tales are, in great measure, biographical and, for that reason, no names have been changed. The reader, therefore, should not be surprised to find that he or some member of his family has an honored place in this book.

PROLOGUE

It has been said that every boy needs a dog. Without intending to challenge the truth of that statement, I say, every boy needs a river. It need not be as large or as important as the Mississippi, as beautiful as the Ohio, nor as powerful as the Niagara. The river I have in mind is none of those. It is a boy-size river. It is one capable of supporting aquatic life, because a boy sometimes needs to go fishing. It has enough water, moving not too swiftly, to allow a flat-bottomed boat to be poled upstream by a young lad with all the ambition, but not the strength, of a full grown man. And, perhaps most importantly, it has places where it is wide enough, deep enough, and sufficiently shielded from view to accommodate the nearest thing to a boy's private Heaven-on-earth, a "swimming hole." I have just introduced you to Mud River.

Mud River begins its journey in a rugged, remote region generally referred to as "Upper Mud River." It flows gently, when not in flood, past the sleepy Town of Hamlin, West Virginia, then on into other parts of Lincoln County, known as "Lower Mud River." Where it goes from there is not a matter of great concern to the local residents, although they are vaguely aware that the natural resource from which its name is derived eventually ends up in the Gulf of Mexico. Mud River is so named because eighty percent of the time it is, in a word, muddy. The rest of the time it has a milky green appearance. But it is never clear and seldom can one see bottom, even in the shallows.

Now that I have acquainted you with Mud River, let me introduce you to the subject of this presentation, the "Mud River Tales." It is a collection of stories in rhyme. They are not about Mud River at all, but about people and events which comprise a great body of memories of times past. Many of them are set in that period of hard times known as the great depression. When I have begun to tell these stories to my children in order to make a point, the response often has been, "Oh no, here comes another depression story." But by dressing them in the garb of poetry and, where appropriate, adding the spice of humor or sentiment, I have succeeded in generating a measure of genuine interest in and appreciation of those times and people and events.

My family moved often when I was a child and we lived on or near many rivers, as is reflected in some of these tales. But it is the Mud River that has remained the focal point of most of them.These are my memories, but not mine exclusively. So read on. Let your mind go where Mud River flows. Allow your memories to mingle with mine. Perhaps you will find that they too are a part of the ***Mud River Tales***.

THE TALES BEGIN

First, let me take you on a short guided tour of the Town of Hamlin, the county seat of Lincoln County. There is a controversy concerning the origin of its name. Some say it was named after a prominent Methodist bishop whose name was Hamline. Others claim that it was named in honor of Hannibal Hamlin, Vice-President during the first term of President Abraham Lincoln, after whom the county was named. The truth cannot be ascertained, because the burning of the courthouse in 1909 destroyed all the pertinent records. However, what follows is not about the town's origin, but mine. It is a look at my hometown.

HOMETOWN

Oh, little Town of Hamlin,
How dear you are to me.
Whether near or far away,
You haunt my reverie.
Those happy scenes of childhood,
Familiar sights and sounds,
Your friendly, smiling faces
Still in my thoughts abound.

In memory I stand again
Atop the "Devil's Head" *
And view your tilted landscape,
Which lies before me spread.
I hear the striking of the clock
Beneath the courthouse dome
And catch Bud Reynolds' whistle
Calling Jack and Jimmie home.

---

* *See, "The Devil's Head" which follows*

I see the form of Grandpa's house
Beyond a row of trees,
With Grandma's wash upon the line
Flapping in the breeze.
Upon that site, old-timers tell,
The town's first cabin stood,
Built by a pioneer hunter
When this was virgin wood.

Across the street, o'ershadowed,
By the Lincoln National Bank,
Ora Washburn's cottage
Of vertical wood plank
Brings to mind the times that we
(And this I shame to tell)
Tossed pebbles on her metal roof
Just to hear her yell.

Farther up the street I see,
Just as it stood before,
The sprawling connected framework
Of the Sweetland General Store,
Where one could buy most anything,
From ink to incubator,
And ride up to the second floor
On a rope-drawn elevator.

The widow Carie Thacker's home
Stands opposite the store.
"Dr. L. M. Thacker" reads
The nameplate on the door.
And the stucco on the corner,
Once the prominent location
Of the Farmers and Merchants Bank,
Is the Board of Education.

Around the corner and beyond
The alley intersection,
At Nora Curry's little store
Of groceries and confection,
We'd meet the bread deliveryman,
At the first stop he would make,
And redeem our saved bread wrappers
For chocolate cupcake.

There too, we'd greet the iceman
And climb upon his truck
To search beneath the heavy tarp
For bits of ice to suck.
Or stand so close as, skillfully,
He'd cut the blocks so true,
To feel the cooling ice-spray,
Which from his ice pick flew.

On farther out the way I see,
By the bus and taxi stop,
The sign of Grandpa's restaurant,
G.L. Pauley's "Coffee Shoppe,"
And next door, the theater
Of the redhead, Maxie Sites,
Where our favorite cowboy heroes
Rode the range on Saturday nights.

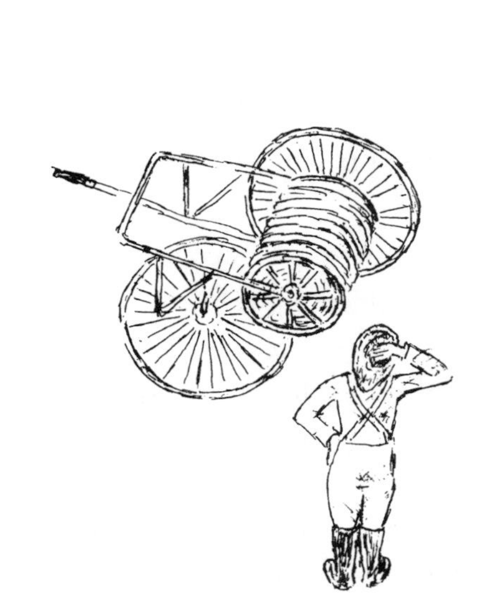

I recall the conflagration,
When the theater went up in smoke.
The fire hose cart was summoned,
But enroute its axle broke.
The theater was destroyed,
And Max was out of luck,
But the townsfolk were persuaded
To buy a fire truck.

There stands the Central M.E. Church
And parsonage next door,
Across from Plumley's Poolroom
And Steffie's Rexall Store.
Kingery's Esso Station stands
On the busiest of corners,
Across from Koontz's Funeral Home,
That's always filled with mourners.

I see the school and football field
Where the Bobcats play to win,
When facing Guyan Valley
O'er that oval of pigskin.
And there, on Independence Day,
Events are always big,
With speeches, fireworks and attempts
To catch a greasy pig.

Down in the lower part of town,
That box-like frame so tall,
Once a thriving flour mill,
Marks the junkyard of Rome Ball,
Where an enterprising youngster,
Who of wit is not too slow,
May convert a wagonload of junk
To the price of a movie show.

An aged, wooden, covered bridge,
An engineering feat,
Spans the waters of the Mud
At the foot of Walnut Street.
What a boyhood thrill to climb
Its massive inclined beam
And from the topmost point to spit
Into that muddy stream.

Mud River taught me how to swim
And how to pole a boat,
To make a crude roof-tin canoe
And keep the thing afloat,
To bait a hook and catch a fish
And how to skip a stone,
And where to go for solitude
When I wished to be alone.

Oh Hamlin, Hamlin, things have changed
From how they used to be.
Gone are those we knew as old
And now the old are we.
The covered bridge, the Sweetland Store
And Grandpa's house, all gone.
A dome-less edifice presides
Upon the courthouse lawn.

Yet while memory remains,
No changes can destroy
The image of the town I knew
When I was just a boy,
Where I still walk in reverie
And tenderly embrace
The spirits that I hold so dear,
Which linger in this place.

When my last beleaguered breath
Escapes this mortal frame,
The striving of this feeble tongue
Will be to speak your name
And bid my swift-departing soul
To pause while upward bound,
For one last look at Hamlin,
My birthplace, my Hometown.

On the highest point of a hill to the west of Hamlin, overlooking the town, lies a large stone on which has been carved a mysterious face. No one living has knowledge of its origin or meaning, but it has been the subject of much speculation. That place is known as "The Devil's Head." I experienced, first hand, the terror of that place one dark, moonless night when a group of older boys took me there on a "snipe" hunting expedition. For the uninitiated, let me explain that snipe hunting is sort of a rite of passage for boys along Mud River. It is also a cruel hoax perpetrated on young boys by older boys, who were subjected to the same cruelty when they were young boys, all in the name of fun. An unsuspecting young lad, honored to have been invited by a group of older boys to participate in one of their activities, is led to a desolate spot on a very dark night. He is then given a burlap bag and told to remain in place, holding it open, while the others in the group round up the snipes and chase them into the bag. The older boys then vanish into the darkness and return to their favorite hangout, leaving their frightened victim "holding the bag." I'm getting up a group to go snipe hunting tonight at the Devil's Head. Want to go? I'll show the way.

THE DEVIL'S HEAD

Cross the covered wooden bridge.
Take the pathway up the hill.
Continue climbing then until
You reach the high point of the ridge.

In that lonely windswept place,
As if by a titan thrown,
Lies a large ungainly stone
With a dreadful graven face.

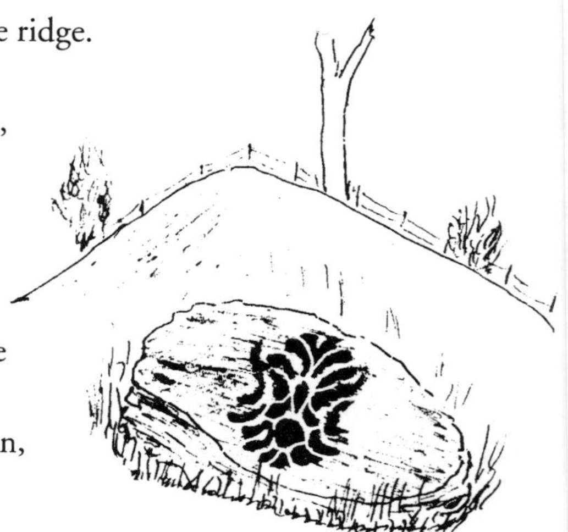

No one knows who put it there
Or how long it thus has lain
Weathered by the wind and rain,
Its silent message to declare.

Perhaps it is a monument
To some long forgotten race,
Which once sojourned in this place
And left it for a testament.

Or, possibly, some mountebank,
Of the stone engravers art,
Carved those features as a part
Of some ancient devilish prank.

Our forefathers viewed with dread
That satanic countenance
And, as a fitting consequence,
Named that place "The Devil's Head."

It has long been quite renown
As a Sunday picnic site.
And its unobstructed height
Provides a birds-eye view of town.

But horror stories do abound
Of bloody sacrificial rites,
Ghostly sounds and eerie lights
And demons rising from the ground.

But don't be cowered or misled.
Boldly cross the covered bridge.
Take the path up to the ridge
And stand upon "The Devil's Head."

Enjoy that awe-inspiring sight.
Pass the day without a care.
And if you're one to take a dare,
Come prepared to spend the night.

During my childhood years, I was privileged to spend much time in my grandfather's house. In fact, I was singularly blessed by having been born in that house, and later, as a result of my mother's untimely demise and my grandfather's intervention, my brother Billy and I returned to live there. I adored my grandfather, and came to love that old house, which seemed an extension of his personality. Even now, I find it difficult to think of one without the other. This is how I remember Grandpa's house.

GRANDPA'S HOUSE

Grandpa's house was a special place,
Endowed with an air of style and grace,
Not elegant, nor yet austere,
Blessed with a friendly atmosphere,
A stately mansion, of highest rank,
Situate just opposite the Hamlin Bank,
A dwelling well suited to a family of ten,
Befitting a teacher and leader of men,
And like its humble dweller, whose character shone,
That house had a character all its own.

The big front door was never locked,
And callers hardly ever knocked.
The glowing mantle of a lone gaslight
Illumined the foyer day and night.
Beveled glass windows, not to be outdone,
Spread a rainbow of color in the evening sun.
Double sliding doors closed the "living room,"
And opened only to admit the broom,
Unless, on special occasions rare,
The family had reason to gather there.

The house had eleven rooms in all,
Not counting the pantry, bath and hall.

Most had a gas-fed fireplace,
With asbestos lining and porcelain face.
There were two staircases, front and back,
With dark oak woodwork, almost black.
The exterior was painted a gleaming white.
No other color seemed quite right.
The broad front porch curved sharply around
And a red metal roof was worn like a crown.

That roof, when touched by the morning sun,
Would ping and bang and pop like a gun.
In the cool of the evening, with night closing in,
The clatter would start all over again.
On severe stormy nights, disturbing to rest,
That roof was at its behavioral best.
In tune to the beat of the falling rain,
The roof would sing a soothing refrain.
With the window raised just above the sill,
That sound was a gentle sleeping pill.

To folks in the lower part of town,
Grandpa's house was "higher ground."
Reason enough to offer thanks,
When Mud River overflowed its banks.
The big front door was opened wide.
The furniture was moved aside.
Beds were laid from wall to wall,
And gentle townsfolk, one and all,
Fleeing from the flood and storm,
Found a refuge safe and warm.

Grandpa's house was the first, I'm told,
To have running water, hot and cold.
From a well in the basement, dark and dank,

Water was lifted to an attic tank,
Whence, by gravity, it would flow
To the kitchen and bath below.
With the coming of a public water supply,
That attic tank, left high and dry,
Became a convenient hiding place,
Where secrets vanished without trace.

The abandoned well a hazard posed,
So the opening had been safely closed
By a great wooden box, weighted with stone,
And all were admonished to leave it alone.
But brother Bill, cousin Jimmie and I
Just couldn't let such a challenge go by.
So, at the first opportunity,
With strength supplied by curiosity,
We moved that box from o'er the well,
And gazed, as it were, into darkest Hell.

Grandpa's house was a child's delight,
Where everything seemed to come out right.
When the weather caused our world to shrink,
The basement became a skating rink.
And the musty attic, with its treasures stored,
Was a pirate's cave to be explored.
There were many things into which to peek,
Ideal spots to hide-and-seek,
And from attic windows' lofty height
Model planes were launched in flight.

From the attic dormer, where we slept,
Brother Billy and I sometimes crept
Out the window and onto the roof,
And, as if courage demanded proof,

We'd climb the steep to the very crown,
Where we had an excellent view of the town.
From that pinnacle we watched in wonder,
As young "Chuck" Yeager, in a bolt of thunder,
To the elders' chagrin and the youngsters delight,
Buzzed the town at treetop height.

I remember well when Grandpa died.
The sliding doors were opened wide.
A special occasion, none too rare,
Brought all his friends and family there,
To pay respects and commemorate
He whose body lay in state.
Throughout the house I knew so well,
Sounds of mourning rose and fell,
Until the thought came o'er me sweeping
That the house itself was weeping.

With Grandpa gone things quickly changed.
Our lives had to be rearranged.
Although Grandma did her best,
She quite candidly confessed
That her income would not sustain
Two growing boys, much less maintain
That big old house she loved so well
And, of necessity, must sell.
So, a sale was made and, brokenhearted,
From Grandpa's house we then departed.

There were occasions, not a few,
When I that house again would view.
And it seemed to me no small disgrace,
That strangers dwelt in Grandpa's place.
Then one snowy winter day,

When late I chanced to pass that way,
There lay, where Grandpa's house had stood,
A rubble of stone and splintered wood,
All that remained, o'er which to mourn,
Of that great house where I was born.

Now, in my garden, standing alone,
There rests an old foundation stone,
Rescued from that snowy debris.
And should one chance to ask of me,
"What is the meaning of that stone?"
My heart shall answer and intone,
It is the remembrance of a man,
Who touched my life as none else can,
A flickering flame that will not douse,
The heart and soul of Grandpa's house.

At one point, near the end of his life, my grandfather was principal of a two-room country school on "Upper Mud River," known as Big Creek School. It was not a great distance from his home at Hamlin and he commuted to school each day. Since my brother Billy and I were residing in his home and in his charge, by his choice, we too attended Big Creek School and traveled with him each day. There was no electric bell or intercom system. The beginning and ending of the school day and other important events were announced by the ringing of the schoolmaster's hand-held brass bell. After a time, we no longer made a distinction between the sound of the bell and the voice of the schoolmaster. The bell was the master's voice. After my grandfather's demise, his house was sold and his books were disposed of. All that remained was the bell, which passed into the possession of his youngest daughter. Could there be a more fitting place to store a prized but unused school bell than a bookcase?

THE SCHOOLMASTER'S BELL

As I the bookcase pass,
Beyond the darkened glass
A gleam of tarnished brass
Gains my attention.
Within that musty cell,
Where faded volumes dwell,
An old schoolmaster's bell
Abides suspension.

Sound yet, as when first cast
From brazier's furnace blast,
In beauty, unsurpassed,
Of tone, well suited
To make the heart rejoice,
And so, became the choice
To speak the master's voice,
A voice now muted.

Enchanted by its spell,
I tap that brazen shell.
At once, a rising swell
Comes ringing.
Did e'er a note so sweet
At my heart's door entreat
Or mem'ries so replete
Come winging?

I see a by-gone day,
A schoolhouse by the way,
Where happy children play,
A school bell pealing,
A pledge with outstretched hand,
A hymn to native land,
A prayer that all may stand
At Truth's revealing.

Then quickly comes to mind
A gentle soul and kind,
To learning much inclined,
An earnest quester,
Who would that all excel,
A teacher loved so well,
The master of the bell,
My own ancestor.

I hear that plaintive knell
In measured cadence swell.
Far over hill and dell
The sound comes ringing,
To summer's end achieve,
From slothfulness retrieve,
From play-time's short reprieve
The children bringing.

When children summoning
From the playground swing,
Soft and gentle its ring,
Ever so tender.
But defiance, arousing ire,
Brings coarser tones and higher,
Ringing coals of fire
On the offender.

In the schoolmaster's hand,
Tolling at his command,
Who could but understand
It was a token
That he who stroked the bell
Wielded the rod as well,
And he on whom it fell
In tears was broken.

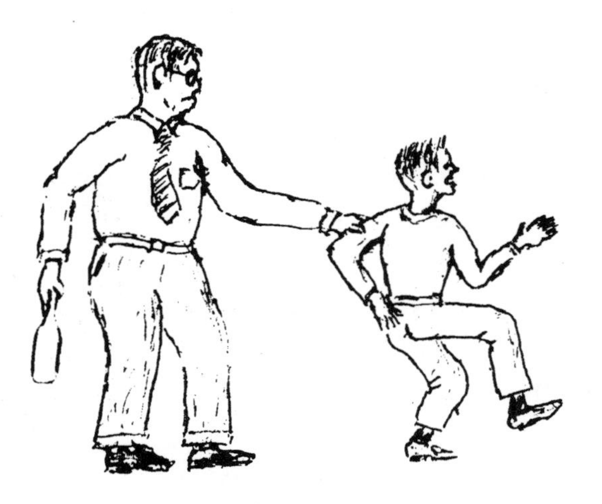

To the master of the school
The bell is but a tool
For discipline and rule
Maintaining.
But as its tones so clear
Fall on the students' ear,
The master's voice they hear
Ordaining.

For four and thirty years
His chosen course he steers,
Respected by his peers,
Highly commended.
An able administrator,
Devoted educator
And teaching innovator,
Well interblended.

Then, as a star expelled,
Bright through the heav'ns propelled,
Is thence no more beheld,
He passed asunder.
He heard the solemn knell
Of a more distant bell,
Summoning him to dwell
In mansions yonder.

Its brassen voice now hushed,
Into the bookcase must,
The master's bell was thrust,
Rudely suspended.
None hears its mute lament
Or knows its discontent.
When will its punishment
Be ended?

When sounds the trumpet blast,
When all of life is past,
Into the fire He'll cast
Both new and old.
Transformed, the bell shall pass
Into the Master's class,
No longer tarnished brass,
But brightest gold.

Grandma always kept chickens. She raised them from tiny chicks which she purchased by mail and kept in a brooder in the basement where they would be safe and warm. When they were large enough she dressed and sold them as fryers. She also kept some laying hens. There were several varieties: Barred Rocks; Rhode Island Reds; and White Leghorns. The most predominant species was Dominique. But we didn't know them by that name. They were always called Dominickers. And, to me, that always spelled trouble.

FOWL PLAY

Grandma's Dominecker hen
Was, with others, kept within
The old garage, with floor suspended,
Complete with chicken yard appended,
Enclosed by fence, six feet or higher,
Of wooden posts and chicken wire.
She gave them tender loving care,
Food and water, light and air,
And watched them fight and scratch and peck
Until the day she'd wring their necks.
Flying was completely banned,
But, lest they didn't understand,
To guard against an errant slip,
One wing per chicken she would clip.
But that old Dominecker hen,
Time and time and time again,
When no one was there to snoop,
Made escape and "flew the coop."
To Bill and me befell the lot
To chase until that bird was caught,
And search the closure all about
To see where she was getting out.
Her exit route was so concealed,
That never was the truth revealed.

As oft as we would put her in,
That hen would slip right out again.
We soon began to tire and sicken
Of that endless game of "chicken."
One morning, Grandpa called us out,
And of the reason left no doubt.
That wayward, speckled hen, said he,
Was out again and running free,
And when last seen was scratching hot
In Grandma's seeded garden spot.
We found the hen and gave her chase.
But she was winning every race,
So Grandpa came to lend a hand.
He told us both to stop and stand
Then move together, cautiously,
And trap that hen between us three.
Since Grandpa was the wiser head,
We did exactly as he said.
But that old bird, no ingenue,
Had crossed the lot a time or two.
In a flash, that hen was gone,
And ere the light on us would dawn,
Had safely reached and taken lodge
Beneath the floor of the garage.
The floor was off the ground, but low,
In the back, a foot or so,
But forward, closing to the ground,
Until no crawling space was found.
About half-way, a wooden beam
Projected downward, so extreme,
As to nearly close the breach.
There stood that hen, just out of reach.
Quick was Grandpa to admit
That in that space he could not fit.

And Billy, always proud to claim
He was more muscular of frame,
Convinced me that my smaller stature
Made me the perfect chicken-snatcher.
So, on a mission I was sent.
To grab that chicken my intent.
But scarcely had I crawled within,
When that old Dominecker hen,
As if to spoil my perfect scheme,
Slipped behind that wooden beam.
There lay darkness, grief and gloom.
I felt a deepening sense of doom.
My mission still yet incomplete,
I was about to sound retreat
When Billy quipped, "Don't be a chicken!"
So on I pressed, near panic-stricken.
Beyond the beam I could not see,
Nor could I reach sufficiently
To grab the hen and pull her through.
There was but one thing I could do.
I pressed my face into the dirt,
Raised all the strength I could exert
And with a will no less supreme,
Forced head and shoulders past the beam.
There, just inches from my chin,
Sat Grandma's Dominecker hen.
Her travel options had expired,
But, for sound, that bird was wired.
Though she had no room to walk,
She exercised her right to squawk.
I grabbed her leg, but cursed my luck,
For then I found that I was stuck
Between that beam and solid ground.
My heart began to loudly pound.

I could not move and I was frantic,
With all the telltale signs of panic.
I cried and screamed and thrashed about,
Convinced that I would ne'er get out.
But though it sounds a bit absurd,
I kept a grip on that old bird.
When Billy recognized my plight
And knew that I was wedged in tight,
He grabbed my legs and pulled me free.
The chicken came along with me.
That hen and I made such a fuss
That Grandma came to check on us.
The hen was none the worse for wear,
But I was bruised from here to there,
And frightened near out of my wits,
Which nearly gave my Grandma fits.
She gave my head a pat or two
And comforted as grandmas do.
She held me close to calm my fears
And with her apron dried my tears.
Grandma said to take the hen
And put her in the coop again,
Though well she knew that, to our grief,
Her home confinement would be brief.
But Grandpa said, "Enough of that."
Then he and Grandma had a chat.
Grandma's order was rescinded,
And as she held that bird upended,
She firmly grasped it by the head.
Then she turned to me and said
That I need never fret again
O'er that old Dominecker hen.
And from the way that Grandma looked,
I knew that chicken's goose was cooked.

We were heroes, Bill and I,
At least in our grandparents' eye.
I had caught that mean old hen.
Bill had saved his brother's skin.
What could such brave acts bespeak?
Chicken and dumplings, "Dominique."
I was proud to be a winner
And have the loser come to dinner,
But prouder then and prouder still
To be the brother of brother Bill.
Yet sometimes in my darkest dream,
I'm stuck again beneath that beam,
And looming o'er me, mean as sin,
Is Grandma's Dominecker hen.

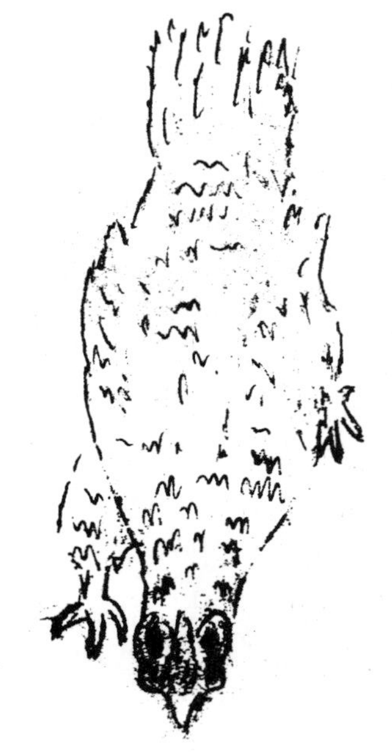

Most of us have a fear of something, usually stemming from an experience in childhood. Some fear the dark; others tight places or heights. With me, it's turkeys, and with good reason.

TURKEY DRESSING

When it came to dressing chickens,
Grandma was the very best.
I suspect that, in her lifetime,
Several thousand birds she dressed,
What with fixing chicken dinners
At the restaurant in town;
Not to mention fresh-dressed fryers
Sold for seven cents a pound.

Now I've never understood it,
(It's a mystery I suppose)
Why one says he's "dressing" chickens
While he's taking off their clothes.
Or why, when speaking about chickens,
One must be so circumspect,
And never say, "Go kill the chicken."
But say instead, "Go wring its neck."

Grandma had a special talent:
She could wring a neck so quick.
Or she'd simply yank the head off,
Held beneath an old broomstick.
The chopping block Grandma avoided.
The axe she always seemed to dread,
Since her sister missed the chicken
And Grandma's finger chopped instead.

Dressing turkeys was her forte,
Which required some finesse,
Because turkeys, unlike chickens,
Oft display aggressiveness.
And you can't just wring their heads off
And then let them flop around,
'Cause the tender meat will damage
As it's bouncing on the ground.

Grandma had devised a system
That was really kind of neat.
She'd up-end and tie that gobbler
To the clothesline by its feet.
Then her butcher-knife appearing,
Would on that creature's neck descend.
And skillfully as any surgeon,
She'd amputate its pecking end.

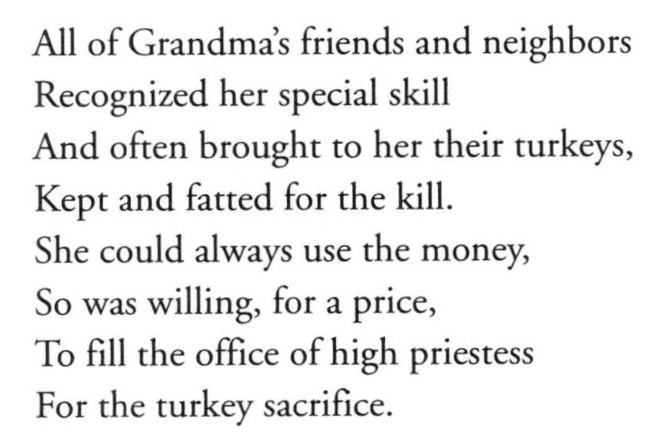

All of Grandma's friends and neighbors
Recognized her special skill
And often brought to her their turkeys,
Kept and fatted for the kill.
She could always use the money,
So was willing, for a price,
To fill the office of high priestess
For the turkey sacrifice.

I remember one Thanksgiving,
When they brought to her nineteen
Of the biggest, meanest turkeys
This tender lad had ever seen.
We kept them under bushel baskets
Or under washtubs overturned,
Or tied to stakes out in the garden
While they briefly there sojourned.

I never really cared for turkeys,
And I viewed them with some dread.
But it often was my duty
To assist when they were fed.
While so engaged, one mean old gobbler,
Escaped and chased me o'er the lot,
Pecking me, I well remember,
On my tender you-know-what.

But my Grandma, quite undaunted,
Taking up her spool of twine,
Soon had nineteen birds inverted,
Swinging from a sagging line.
They at once became quite docile,
And content as newly-weds.
But when her butcherknife descended,
They completely lost their heads.

Suddenly, those birds exploded.
Turkey feathers filled the air.
On that clear November morning,
Red raindrops fell everywhere.
Grandma seemed to take no notice.
I looked on as in a trance,
While those nineteen headless turkeys
Did a grotesque high-wire dance.

In the Bible, 'tis recorded
How the ancient Israelites,
For their sins did seek atonement
Through bloody sacrificial rites.
Blood of bulls and goats won't save us,
Says the Word, and I agree,
But those nineteen headless turkeys
Made a believer out of me.

Now, in the supermarket cooler,
Trimmed and packaged, oh so neat,
Freshly dressed Thanksgiving turkey
Is just another kind of meat.
But in my mind, I always see them
Dancing headless on the line,
So when you say, "Please have some turkey,"
Pardon me if I decline.

Every town has its characters: those whose manner of dress, lifestyle and behavior mark them as somewhat outside the norm. They are often regarded as corrupting influences. Young folk are admonished to avoid them and not follow their example. Yet, they never seem to lack for friends and are often seen as possessing special talents and abilities which are lacking in those who sit in judgment of them.

JESSE PLAYED THE FIDDLE

From the lower end of town,
Where Mud River makes a bend,
In the evening, about sundown,
I could hear a violin.

The music captured my attention
And caused my heart to quicken pace.
But Grandma, sensing my intention,
Said, "Stay away from Jesse's place."

His place was on the edge of town,
Hard upon the River Mud.
It always looked a bit rundown,
So oft had it endured the flood.

Although in need of much repair,
There was reason for delay,
For when the Mud went on a tear,
Jesse's house was in the way.

Jesse worked when'er it suited,
Not at all when so inclined.
Were laziness to him imputed,
Jesse didn't seem to mind.

And when the evening sun was low,
Upon his front porch Jesse stood

With his fiddle and his bow
And entertained the neighborhood.

Jesse had a reputation
For that which some equate with sin:
Drinking to intoxication,
A little bootlegging now and then.

To top it off, he played the fiddle;
The Devil's invention, some would say.
In Grandma's eyes, more than a little
Cause for me to stay away.

But Grandma's warning went unheeded,
Though I tried to be discreet.
The fiddle called me and I needed
To hear it played at Jesse's feet.

So, I sometimes was observed,
As twilight turned another page,
Seated on the porch that served
As Jesse's fiddle concert stage.

Accompanied by a kindred spirit
On the banjo or guitar,
Nearly all the town could hear it,
Jesse's fiddle rang afar.

When he played "Fire on the Mountain,"
You could almost feel the heat.
With the tempo ever mounting,
Folks would start to move their feet.

He played "Billy in the Low Ground,"
"Sally Goodin" and "Old Joe Clark,"
"Soldier's Joy" and "Chinese Breakdown,"
Fiddling long into the dark.

When no longer could I tarry,
Sadly to my room I'd creep.
With my window wide and airy,
He would fiddle me to sleep.

I heard that Jesse got religion
And gave up all his sinful ways
And, as a sign of deep contrition,
Swore off the fiddle all his days.

I suppose that solves the riddle,
Why the deeply moving sound
Of Jesse's sweet-voiced singing fiddle
Was no longer heard in town.

Mud River still does not forbear
To spill, at times, into the town.
But Jesse's house need not despair,
For long ago it was torn down.

Now Jesse has another place,
Upon a far and distant shore,
With a porch and concert space,
Where he can fiddle evermore.

But sometimes in the eventide,
When the shadows softly creep,
With my window open wide
And I am drifting off to sleep,

I feel my heart begin to pound
And to quicken pace a little,
As my ears pick up the sound
Of Jesse's distant ringing fiddle.

Mud River is not regarded as one of the more romantic streams. I don't recall having heard a song about it nor, to my knowledge, has it been described as beautiful. It is not the kind of river that evokes strong feelings. You might say that it is rather benign. True, like some people I know, it sometimes goes on a binge and does some terrible things, but then it repents and all is forgiven. In fact, at times, it actually seems to have a spiritual side.

THE BAPTIZING

March came in much warmer
Than any could remember.
The heavy snows which decked the ground
Since early in December
Had turned to slush, then disappeared,
In that unseemly heat.
And on the sunbaked pavement
Children walked with barren feet.

Over in the Baptist Church
Things were really hot.
The preacher stirred the fires of hell
And warned, "This be the lot
Of those who worldly pleasures seek
And are by sin enslaved."
That was the Sunday, I recall,
The Bailey girl "got saved."

There were amens from the corner.
Great tears of joy were shed.
Then, at the benediction,
The preacher 'rose and said,
"We know the time is nearing.
His coming may be soon.
So let's baptize this little one
This very afternoon."

Soon that little congregation
Of forty souls or more
Had gathered at Mud River
Behind the Sweetland Store.
A place that was familiar
To every kid in town,
Where boys went skinny-dippin'.
When no one was around.

The preacher led the group in prayer,
Then boldly waded in,
Escorting the young lady
'Till the water touched her chin.
He lowered her beneath the wave
And raised her up again,
"In the name of the Father and the Son
And the Holy Ghost, Amen."

They hurried from the water,
There was no hesitating,
Assisted by the deacons,
Who stood with blankets waiting.
Quickly then, the crowd dispersed,
Leaving there behind
Just me, Cousin Jim, and my brother Bill,
Who had something on his mind.

The crowd was hardly out of sight
When Billy said to Jim,
"If it's warm enough for dunkin',
It's warm enough to swim."
With that, he pulled off all his clothes
And bade us do the same.
But sensing our reluctance,
He taunted with a name.

"The last one in's a you-know-what,"
Bill cried as in he went.
He didn't really say the word,
But we knew what he meant.
He came up somewhere near midstream
And gave a thumbs-up sign,
Then added this assurance,
"Come on in, the water's fine."

It didn't take me long to learn
That Bill exaggerated,
For when I dove beneath the wave
I was refrigerated.
The water was so very cold,
It chilled me to the bone
And sent my body temperature
Into the Arctic zone.

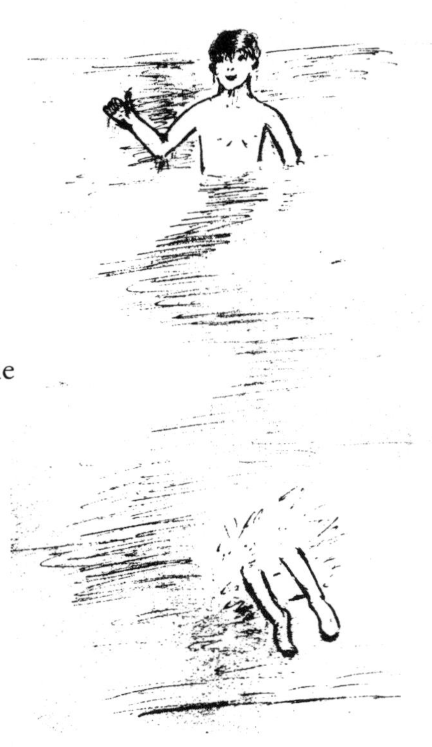

I rushed out of the water,
Shivering from head to toe,
Grabbed my clothes and ran for home
As fast as I could go.
The remainder of the afternoon
I laid out in the sun,
Convinced I'd ne'er again be warm
And feeling quiet outdone.

I wondered how that fragile girl,
The weaker sex I'm told,
Could calmly wade into the stream
When the water was that cold.
Bur grandma always said that she
Was baptized in December,
And it didn't bother her at all,
As well she could remember.

And Grandpa used to break the ice
To take his morning dip.
From those two sturdy oaks
I always thought I was a chip.
But something in the genes, I think,
Got lost in the transmission.
How else could I explain
My cold intolerant condition.

Now, I believe baptizin'
In a river's really cool.
It seems a bit more biblical
Than an indoor heated pool.
But it takes a special person,
Not tainted with cold blood,
To be baptized in winter
In the waters of the Mud.

Folks along Mud River seem to prefer pork to other kinds of meat. They are practical people, and pork is a practical kind of meat. A chicken's principal function is to lay eggs, and it becomes meat only when the preacher comes to Sunday dinner. A cow is prized for its capacity to produce milk. It is consumed as beef on rare occasions, such as, when it is struck by lightning. But hog meat is for every day consumption. Bacon, ham, sausage, pork chops, tenderloin; it's all in there. A hog has but one major function, to produce meat. And it requires less space and is usually less costly to raise than other animals. So, along the river and up the hollows you will often see and experience, in an olfactory way, the family pigpen. And in early winter you may observe and possibly participate in an annual event known as "hog killin' day."

HOG KILLIN' DAY

Bud, the father of Jack and Jim,
Who grew to look a lot like him,
Was tall and rugged and strong of arm,
With a grin broadfaced and warm.
All who knew him called him "Bud."
He lived upon the River Mud
With his good wife Angeline,
Two sons, five daughters, a family of nine.
His aged father made it ten;
Three generations living in
A cottage small that was never meant
To house so many, yet content.

Bud taught his children how to mind.
He was firm but not unkind.
He demanded that they heed his call
And be at home before nightfall.
He had a loud two-finger whistle
That traveled like a far-flung missile.

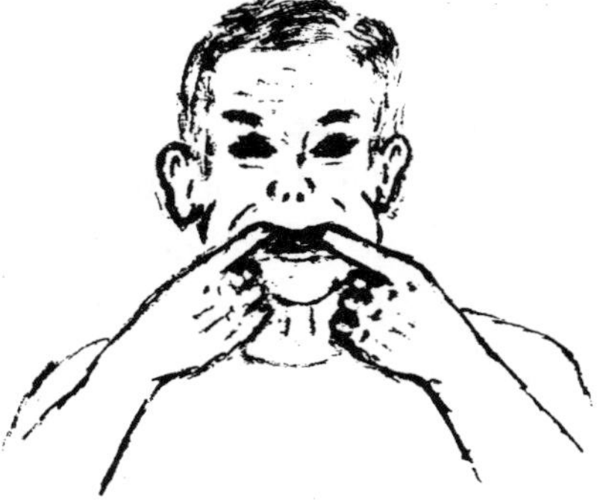

And in late evening, about sundown,
That sound was heard all over town.
Then Jack and Jim would hear and heed
And dart for home at breakneck speed.

By honest toil Bud earned his bread
And always kept his family fed.
But there were many mouths to feed
And pay unequal to the need.
So he kept a pig or two,
Which Jack and Jim attended to.
With table scraps, hog weeds and swill,
The pigs were fatted for the kill.
And, in hard times, he thus was able
To put some meat upon his table.

Bud was no stranger to hard work,
Nor would he his duty shirk,
A trait acquired from his dad:
Bud always gave it all he had.
So, I confess, I was surprised
To learn of work that Bud despised
When, solemnly, I heard him state,
"One day in life I truly hate;
A day to me that is accursed:
Hog killin' day, of all, the worst."

It just so happened, next Saturday,
Bud had declared "hog killin' day."
And I was curious to know,
Just why that day Bud hated so.
So on that day, I vowed I would
Observe and help as best I could.

I arrived at a quarter of eight,
But found that I was hours late,
For Bud, his dad, and Jack and Jim
Had been at work since five A.M.

In a clearing, briar free,
Close by a sturdy low-limbed tree,
They had built a smoking fire,
Which Jack and Jimmie's old grandsire
Was tending in a shallow pit,
An open barrel on top of it,
That, pail by pail, young Jack and Jim
Had filled with water to the brim.

Bud had brought a wooden sled
To haul that hog once it was dead.
He also brought a gun, an axe,
A pile of burlap "coffee sacks,"
A block and tackle, a singletree,
Butcher knives, painstakingly,
Sharpened to a razor's edge,
A length of rope, a tub, a sledge,
All this, and more, made up the rig
To slaughter one young fatted pig.

The water barrel began to boil;
Time then the pigsty to despoil.
Bud knocked the side out of the shed
To make an opening for the sled.
He coaxed that porker with some grain
And put a bullet in its brain,
Then quickly leaped into the mud
And stuck him deep to draw the blood.

That critter, standing on all four,
Had weighed four hundred pounds or more.
But limp and lifeless and undone,
It seemed to weigh at least a ton.
Bud could not move that hog alone,
Nor Jack and Jimmie on their own.
It took the three of them instead
To get the hog upon the sled.

Then Jack and Jim, myself and Bud
Pulled the sled out of the mud
And over by the barrel we hauled
That carcass, ready for the scald.
The hog remained upon the sled
As burlap bags were thickly spread,
'Till every inch of bristled skin
Was blanketed from tail to chin.

The scalding water was applied,
Dipped and poured upon its hide,
The burlap blanket saturating
And clouds of vapor generating,
Much as a barber's towels abide
Before the lather is applied,
Thus the subject to prepare
By softening the skin and hair.

Laying off the burlap draping,
Jack and Jim began the scraping.
Those butcher knives removed the bristle
Slick as Bud's two-finger whistle.
When one side had been completed,
The entire process was repeated
As they then addressed the hide
Of that critter's other side.

Under Bud's attentive eye,
The head, the tail, each leg and thigh
Were groomed till he was satisfied
The hog was ready for "the ride."
Then Jack and Jim and Bud and me
Pulled the sled beneath the tree
Where hung Bud's block and tackle rig,
Prepared to elevate the pig.

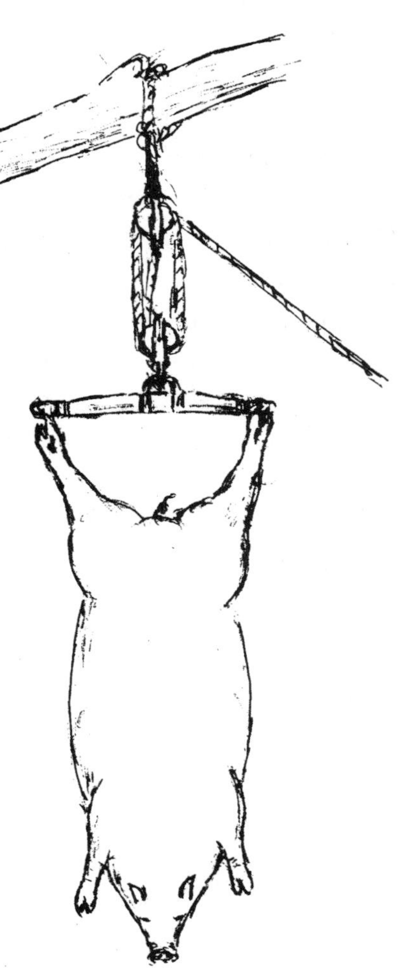

In each hind leg Bud undertook
To place a sturdy metal hook,
Which by a length of chain then he
Connected to the singletree.
And to the balanced center shackle
He attached the block and tackle.
Then every hand was on the rope,
With all our strength to pull and grope
Until the hog was off the sled
And hanging by a slender thread.

Bud his sharpest knife selected
And that pork belly then dissected.
One long cut from stem to stern,
And we its innards could discern.
Then into several big lard pails
He emptied out its great entrails.
Around the neck his big knife sped,
Lopping off that creature's head.
Likewise a cut about the tail
Left both ends lying in a pail.

To some, this rather graphic scene
May appear somewhat obscene

Or cruel, from some points of view,
But Bud did what he had to do.
For ne'er could he by being sweet,
Entice that hog to give its meat.
And if there were another way,
There wouldn't be hog killing day.

What happened next was unforeseen;
A real life tragi-comic scene,
Which rivals, maybe even tops,
The antics of the "Keystone Cops."
To get what's known as a pork side,
One must the carcass first divide.
Connecting tissue must be slit,
Then the backbone neatly split.

Bud instructed Jim and Jack
To hold the belly tissues back.
Then with his pole axe in his reach,
He boldly stepped into the breach.
Bud put his strength into the throw
And gave the spine a mighty blow.
The axe struck squarely on the line,
Embedding in the creature's spine.

The suddenness of his attack
Somewhat startled Jim and Jack.
The belly flesh slipped from their grasp
And instantly did Bud enclasp.
The anchor rope began to slip,
The block and tackle lost its grip
And, all at once, that headless hog
Toppled like a hollow log.

Not in my years, by day or night,
Have I encountered such a sight.
That hog lay quivering in the mud,
Its innards then replaced by Bud.
Where lately grew that hog's great head,
There were feet with shoes instead.
Bud's head, his grin replaced by fear,
Protruded from that porker's rear.

I was completely taken aback.
So too, I think, were Jim and Jack.
For a moment, as time divides,
We laughed and held our splitting sides.
But Bud, confined in innard space,
Could not escape that hog's embrace.
So, while their grandpa stood agog,
Jack and Jimmie rolled the hog
And Bud, befuddled and befouled,
From that hog was disemboweled.

Despite that harrowing affair,
Bud was none the worse for wear.
But he thought it asinine
That he was bested by a swine.
There was no reason he could see
To put that hog back on the tree.
So the spine was split instead
As it lay upon the sled.

The slaughter would not be complete
'Til there remained but cuts of meat.
As Jack and Jimmie held and levered,
The hams and shoulders were dissevered.

The rest Bud later would divide
Into fatback, loin and side,
To be salted and preserved,
Then upon his table served.

There was meat for every taste
And none of it would go to waste.
For pork has such a wide appeal,
That nought is lost, except the squeal.
There was never food to spare,
But with his neighbors Bud would share.
And for my part in that travail,
He presented me the tail.

As I trudged my homeward way,
I thought of what transpired that day.
I had come that I might know
Why that day Bud hated so.
I learned that it was grueling work,
Which many would incline to shirk,
Involving an unpleasant chore,
With grisly scenes of blood and gore.

Such unpleasantness, thought I,
Surely was the reason why
That Bud approached with such dismay
The ordeal of hog killing day.
But from the vantage now of years,
Another point of view appears.
The sum of life's experience
Has given me another sense.

One has but to understand:
That gentle giant of a man,

A simple man, without pretense,
Held all life in reverence
And would desire no harm at all
To any creature, great or small.
Such a man would rue the day
It became his lot to slay.

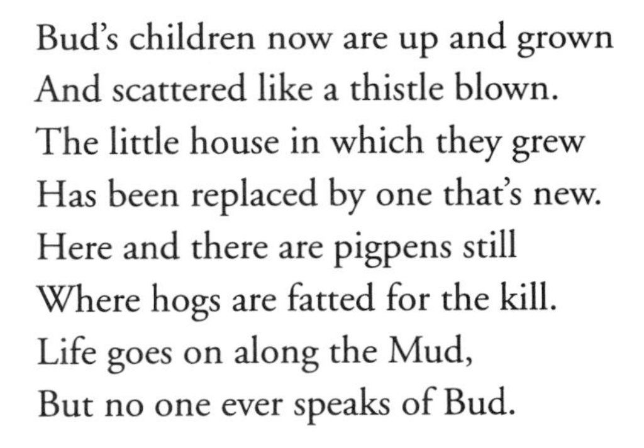

But, in this rugged mountain land,
It is expected of a man
That he learn to shoot and kill,
And thus his family's larder fill.
Nor is it thought a thing so big
For a man to slay a pig.
So how could Bud then not afford
To do the thing he so abhorred?

Bud's children now are up and grown
And scattered like a thistle blown.
The little house in which they grew
Has been replaced by one that's new.
Here and there are pigpens still
Where hogs are fatted for the kill.
Life goes on along the Mud,
But no one ever speaks of Bud.

Bud's great two-finger whistle sound
No longer can be heard in town.
Another whistle caught his ear,
And he responded without fear,
Then hurried home to join his dad.
And I suspect that he was glad
To know that there across the way,
There'd be no more "hog killin' day."

In a town as small and quiet and out-of-the-way as Hamlin, very little happens that can be considered exciting. Of course, there was the time that Jimmy Phillips took off down the Calvin Hall Hill in his crude homebuilt glider. That was exciting, at least up to the point where he crashed and broke his leg. When the movie theatre burned and fire trucks were summoned from as far away as Milton and Huntington because it looked for a while like the whole block would go up in smoke, some folks got real excited. My acquaintance with airplanes had been limited to watching a tiny speck in the sky drone from horizon to horizon. Not much exciting about that. But when a big-as-life airplane with a real emergency is forced to land in a nearby cornfield, that's excitement!

THE AIRPLANE CAME DOWN

It was almost dark when it flew o'er the house
And circled above the town.
We barely had time to run outside
Before it came back around.
Throttled back and descending, it headed west,
Passing low o'er the Sweetland Store,
Then across Mud River, barely clearing the trees
Which lined the opposite shore.

"It crashed, it crashed," I heard someone say,
As townsfolk began to congregate,
Then to hurry on foot up the blacktop road,
The tragedy to investigate.
Brother Billy and I went along with the crowd,
Which included nearly half the town,
In anticipation of our very first glimpse
Of an airplane on the ground.

We crossed Mud River in fading twilight,
Single file on a foot-log bridge,

And found ourselves in a narrow cornfield
Ascending to a sloping ridge.
There we saw the grounded plane,
And its pilot nearby standing.
It had not crashed, as had been supposed,
But had made an emergency landing.

The pilot, a U.S. Navy flier,
On a cross-country training flight,
Off course and low on gasoline,
Had been forced to land for the night.
In his sheepskin-lined leather flying togs,
Appropriate to his flying machine,
He was every inch the aviator
So often portrayed on the screen.

The aircraft, an open cockpit type,
A bi-plane, with struts and wires,
Was the kind of plane quite often flown
By barnstormers and stunt flyers.
It apparently had suffered no real harm
As through the cornfield it plowed,
But the pilot expressed no small concern
That it might be crushed by the crowd.

The county sheriff arrived on the field
And, holding official sway,
Posted a guard o'er the aeroplane
To keep the crowd away.
Then he took the pilot into town
To arrange for some gasoline.
So, groping our way in the dark of night,
We reluctantly left the scene.

Billy and I were up at dawn,
Having hardly slept all night,
Determined that we would be the first
To arrive at the landing site.
But, to our surprise, a burgeoning crowd
Had already begun to convene.
All come to witness the historic flight
Of that fallen flying machine.

The sun was already high in the sky
When the pilot arrived on the scene,
Followed by men from a distant airport
With the much needed gasoline.
They fueled and checked the aeroplane,
All the while continuing to warn,
That a take-off was impossible
From that little field of corn.

The pilot inspected the entire field
And found it soft and rough.
Stopped by the ridge and hemmed by trees,
It just wasn't long enough.
The sloping ridge was firm and straight,
Though covered by bush and thorn.
Its length seemed hardly adequate
To get the plane airborne.

But several men with scythes and axes,
Working in a rush,
Soon had cleared that narrow ridge
Of briers, weeds and brush.
Then eager hands of men and boys,
Tugging on a rope,
Pulled the aircraft from the field
And backed it up the slope.

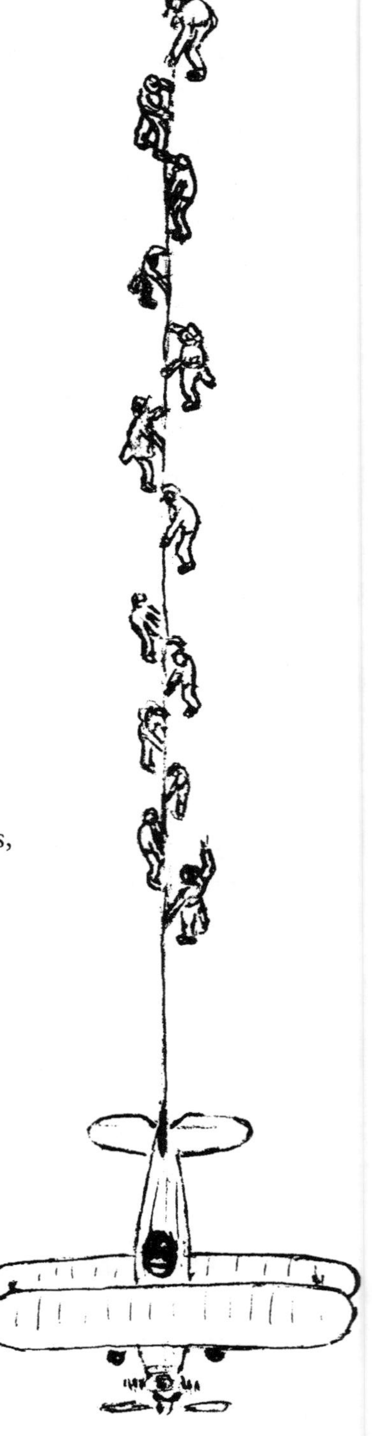

The pilot walked to the precipice
Where the ridge abruptly ended
And knew that ere he reached that point,
The plane must have ascended.
His first attempt would be the last.
The runway was so short,
Once he began his take-off roll,
There'd be no chance to abort.

The pilot made one final check
Then to the cockpit mounted.
All arguments against the flight,
He repeatedly discounted.
The crowd was warned to clear the ridge
And avoid the prop-wash blast.
With a cough the engine roared to life,
The moment had come at last.

The spinning propeller clawed the air,
In eagerness for flight,
While a dozen men determinedly
Restrained with all their might.
With the engine running at full speed,
Building power for the start,
The airplane did a violent dance
'Till it seemed 'twould break apart.

At a signal from the pilot given,
The men their grasp released.
The airplane lunged into its roll,
And swiftly its speed increased.
Like a rabbit flushed from hiding,
Like a startled antelope,
Like a racehorse in the homestretch,
It thundered down the slope.

In less time than it takes to tell,
It took the ridge in stride,
Then, as an arrow's flight is spent,
Began a downward slide.
It never lifted from the ground.
The ground just fell away.
A hush of fear swept o'er the crowd,
And some were heard to pray.

It seemed to all that pilot and plane
Would surely come to grief,
But lo, those wings began to rise
On a great sigh of relief.
At once the silent fearful crowd
Released a joyful cry,
As the airplane lifted o'er the trees
And headed for the sky.

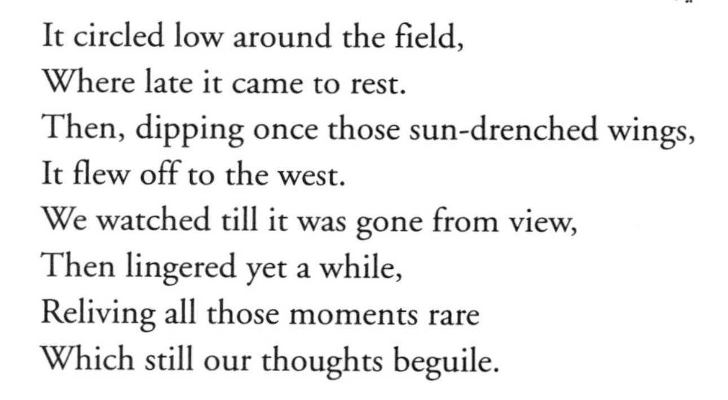

It circled low around the field,
Where late it came to rest.
Then, dipping once those sun-drenched wings,
It flew off to the west.
We watched till it was gone from view,
Then lingered yet a while,
Reliving all those moments rare
Which still our thoughts beguile.

Other wings would buzz our town
And rouse it from its nap
Then usher in the sonic boom
Which placed it on the map.
But if one moment in history
May wear a shining crown,
'Twould be that most exciting time
When that aeroplane came down.

It is widely known that Charles E. "Chuck" Yeager, World War II flying ace and the first man to fly faster than the speed of sound, hails from the Town of Hamlin, West Virginia. His exploits have made him a national hero and a legend in his own time. In his hometown and state he has been honored in many ways. But his first flying visit to his hometown brought him as much criticism as acclaim. This is the recollection of one enthralled eyewitness to that event.

CLOSE ENCOUNTER WITH A HOMETOWN BOY

"Mercy," Grandma cried aloud,
Throwing up her hands,
As a frightening noise engulfed the house,
Rattling her pots and pans.
"What was that?" I heard her ask,
But gave her no reply,
For Billy and I were out the door,
Our eyes glued to the sky.

We knew immediately that sound,
That droning, staccato roar,
As the voice of a powerful engine
Of an aircraft made for war.
For we had heard it oft before
At a Saturday matinee,
As courageous fighter pilots
Rose up to save the day.

The air was saturated
With that airplane's taunting sound.
Yet, it seemed to us invisible
As it swooped in o'er the town,
For a morning mist, suspended,
Withheld it from our view.
"To the roof!" cried brother Billy,
And into the house we flew.

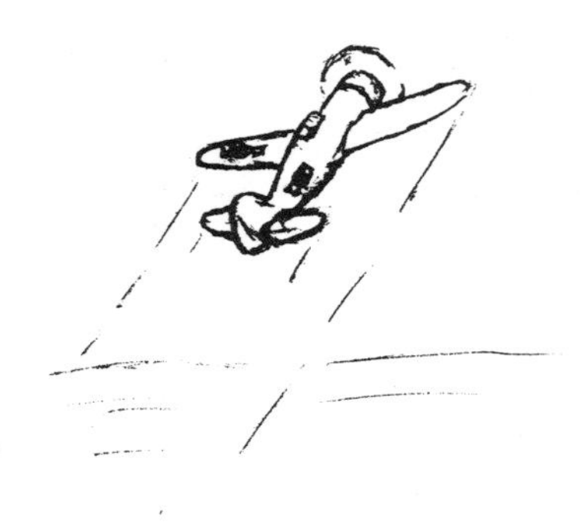

We bolted up the attic stairs
And crawled onto the roof
Then clambered to the very top,
From danger quite aloof.
But, lo, no airplane could we see,
Nor engine could we hear,
As though the plane had gone away,
Or so it did appear.

But, suddenly, with deafening roar,
The sight we sought so much,
Burst through the mist above our heads,
So close, almost to touch.
Vapor trails, like penciled lines,
Streamed from its wings and tail.
From underneath, its fuselage
Seemed like a soaring whale.

Bill and I had studied well
The "Airplane Spotters' Guide"
And could distinguish friend or foe
By profiles, top and side.
Instantly, we recognized
That cigar-shaped sky rider
As a P-47 "Thunderbolt,"
The world's most powerful fighter.

The mist then dissipated
As the sun came shining through,
And from our perch atop the roof
We had a thrilling view.
The airplane crossed the Sweetland Store,
Flying at treetop height,
Then climbed into the morning sun
And disappeared from sight.

The hillsides caught that engine's sound
And echoed their response,
Until the airplane seemed to come
From everywhere at once.
When we were sure that it was there,
Beyond the "Devil's Head,"
It suddenly burst into view
From somewhere else instead.

The Central M.E. Church's spire
Stood helpless in its path.
We watched with bated breath to see
That steeple feel its wrath.
But banking vertically its wings,
It passed the steeple by,
Then thundered o'er the covered bridge
And once more pierced the sky.

Out in the other end of town,
As neighbors watched aghast,
Hal Yeager's white frame residence
It closely overpassed
Then did a climbing victory roll
Above the courthouse dome,
Leaving none in town to doubt
"Chuck" Yeager had come home.

It took a while to realize
The plane had gone away.
We strained to hear that engine's sound
For yet much of the day.
And when we had returned to earth,
We faced Grandma's reproof
For doing such a dangerous thing
As climbing on the roof.

That "Thunderbolt," true to its name,
Had jarred the town awake,
And ushered in the raging storm
Which lingered in its wake.
Grandma said, "He should be whipped
For scaring folks like that."
Said one, "That's just what I'd expect
From that young Yeager brat."

"If he were here," another piped,
"I'd give that kid what for!"
Said others, "Let him have his day,
He's off to fight a war."
The younger folks were thrilled and awed
That "Chuck," their hometown peer,
Had become the modern equal
Of a dashing cavalier.

These attitudes had little changed
When, once the war was won,
He did a hometown encore
In a sleek P-51.
Then later, in a "Shooting Star,"
He pushed the limit some.
Yet we were largely ignorant
Of the hero he'd become.

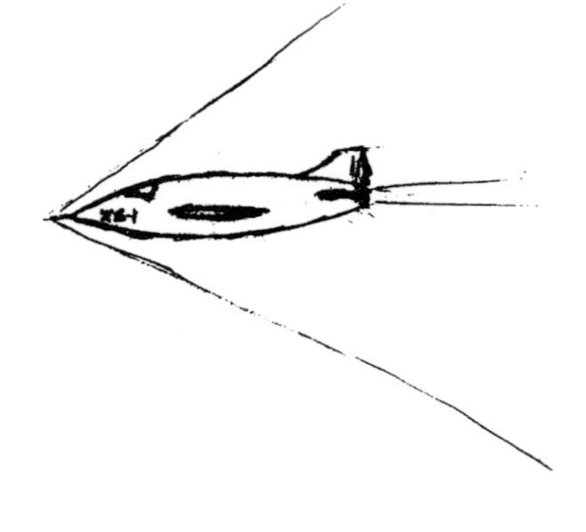

But when he had completed
His supersonic ride,
The entire town of Hamlin
Would point to him with pride
As a genuine folk hero
And to the world expound,
"We're from the town of Hamlin,
Chuck Yeager's old hometown."

Chuck oft has demonstrated
He has all the "right stuff."
Memorials declare it
And they are right enough.
But of all his daring exploits,
None brought to me such joy
As that brief rooftop encounter
With another hometown boy.

Anyone can be a hero. There are no prescribed qualifications for the position. One cannot, by study or special training, gain the stature of hero. Nor is it necessarily a matter of courage, although heroes often act courageously. I do not subscribe to the tenet that heroes are born, that is, born to be heroes and cannot be otherwise. No, heroes are ordinary people who, when faced with a situation which requires action, act, while others, out of concern for their own safety or loss, possible embarrassment or inability to decide upon the right thing to do, are frozen into inaction. Yet, heroes are often embarrassed by their own deeds.

THE RESCUE

It was a steaming afternoon
In the middle of July.
Not a breeze was blowing.
No clouds were in the sky.
Hardly anything was stirring
In that indecent heat,
Except the blacktop pavement,
Which moved beneath our feet.

There was brother Bill and I,
And Gene and Jack and Jim.
Since Billy was the oldest,
We sort of looked to him
To take the lead in planning
The things that we would do.
When Bill said, "Let's go swimming."
We answered, "we're with you."

We set out for the swimming-hole,
A quarter-mile away,
Where we'd been already
Several times that day.

First, up the blacktop roadway,
Past the Thacker cemetery,
Then left, along a weed-choked path,
To that hidden sanctuary.

We dropped our clothing on the bank
But spent no time in sunning.
Dressed only in our broadest grins,
We hit the water running.
Suddenly, there came to ear
The sound of voices nearing,
Then six young girls in bathing suits
Broke forth into the clearing.

We had no time to grab our clothes
Or see to other needs,
But hastily concealed ourselves
Within a patch of weeds.
That is, except my brother Bill,
Who was stubborn as a mule.
"No bunch of silly girls," said he,
"Can chase me from this pool."

The girls appeared to range in age
From ten to early teen,
And though it was quite innocent,
It looked a bit obscene,
To see them there cavorting,
Which some would view as lewd,
Watched closely from the weed-patch
By four boys in the nude.

They didn't seem to mind at all
That Bill remained in view.

But as they moved into the stream,
He quietly withdrew.
Then one fair little maiden,
Who seemed to have no dread,
Ventured out too far from shore
And stepped in o'er her head.

The girls began to panic
And loudly screamed at him
To please go out and save her,
For none of them could swim.
This desperate situation
Bill could not long ignore,
So he sped to the rescue
And carried her to shore.

It soon became apparent,
The girl was quite unharmed,
Though she was somewhat shaken,
And Bill was quite disarmed.
As the maidens gathered 'round him
To express their gratitude,
He forgot, for just a moment,
That he was in the nude.

When Bill came to his senses,
His one thought was to flee,
So he dove into the water
To retrieve his modesty.
The girls then gathered up their things
And quickly left the scene,
Allowing we four nudists
To leave our weed-patch screen.

Bill was quite embarrassed
By the way it all came down,
And swore us all to secrecy,
But the story got around.
When someone broached the subject,
He would stare and fume and fuss,
And say it was a matter
He'd rather not discuss.

By rescuing that little girl
Bill won himself some fame.
Now folks around the county
All know him by his name.
One question they all ask him
Is "Bill, how do you dress,
When you go forth to rescue
A damsel in distress?"

My father was the oldest of eight children and the "runt" of the family. All his brothers stood six feet or more while dad was barely five-six. He quit school, by his own choice, at an early age and, though able to read and write, had a limited education, which restricted his occupational opportunities. Though small of stature, he was a hard worker and would try anything. During his lifetime he was a coal miner, road equipment operator, oil field tool dresser, construction laborer, bartender, truck driver, laundry delivery man, paper mill worker, newspaper deliveryman, and many others. He was regarded as friendly and had many friends, but he had a lifelong weakness for alcohol, which often caused him to stumble and brought much grief to his family. Nevertheless, he was a man of high values and principles, who loved his children and did his best to provide for them. He acknowledged his failings and admonished others not to follow his example. Still, in many ways he was worthy of emulation.

DADDY BANKED THE FIRES

My father could hardly claim
To be a man of wealth or fame,
No stocks or bonds or bank account,
Nor income in a large amount,
No deeds of valor, no great invention,
No skills or talents I could mention,
Save one, for none stood higher
Than my father when he banked the fire.

He had a penchant for strong drink,
And other vices too, I think;
Some character traits considered strong:
Honest as the day is long;
And friendly, which did friends beget;
'Twas said he ne'er a stranger met,
But more than friend; he was my sire,
And with a father's love he banked the fire.

He left for the mines before the dawn
And returned long after light was gone,
So weary that he could do no more
Than to bathe himself by the kitchen door.
So brother and I did what we could:
I carried in coal; he chopped the wood.
Together we kept the home fires bright,
But it was dad who banked the fires at night.

For he had the thought, and perhaps he was right,
That a man's worth is measured, not by riches or might,
Nor by victories won or by seeds he has sown,
But how a man provides for his own.
And he had no kind words for a lazy lout,
Who, by neglect, would let his fire go out.
This responsibility he could not share,
So Daddy banked the fires with special care.

After the evening chores were done
And the children had been bathed, one by one,
After the prayers had all been said,
And we lay snuggling and shivering in our bed,
I would see my father's shadowy frame
Loom large before the flickering flame.
Then like a music master directing a choir,
He skillfully, lovingly, banked the fire.

He shook the ashes to the hearth below.
Then stirred the coals to a golden glow.
As he fed more coal for a fuel bed,
The flames leaped up, flashing blue and red.
Then a coating of coal dust would sizzle and pop
'Till smothered by a blanket of ashes on top.
An occasional flare was a welcome sight,
For he knew then the fire would last the night.

My dad was short and rather slim.
Some folks say I look a lot like him.
And sometimes in my mirror I think I see
My father gazing back at me.
I loved that man, maybe most of all,
But if ever I told him, I can't recall.
And I wonder sometimes, when I prepare to retire,
Would he approve of the way I bank the fire?

For a long time now I've been on my own,
And I have children already grown.
They don't remember my dad at all,
'Cause he died when they were very small.
But I tell them about him, both the good and the bad.
Some stories are funny, some kind of sad.
But the one that fills them with delight
Is how Daddy banked the fires at night.

It was a recurring theme in movies about the old west. Men who had gone west to seek their fortunes and, finding a scarcity of women on the frontier, paid large sums for mail order brides, sight unseen. I always found it a little hard to believe that a single woman would endure the hardships and dangers of a two thousand mile trip by wagon across the country just to marry a man whom she had never met and about whom she knew nothing. But what my mother did to get a husband was not so very different.

MOMMA BOUGHT A HUSBAND

Some girls can get a husband
Just by being coy and sweet,
While some rely on wit and charm
To sweep him off his feet.
Others, more domestic,
Skilled in culinary art,
Profess that through the stomach
Lies the pathway to the heart.

A few resort to trickery,
To subterfuge and guile,
To trap an unsuspecting groom
And march him down the aisle.
But Mom's approach was different,
Though by some standards brash.
She bought herself a husband
With her own hard-earned cash.

Momma had been married
Before she married Dad.
Her husband was a callous,
Unmitigated cad.
He abandoned wife and daughter
Without the least remorse.

So that ill-fated marriage
Had ended in divorce.

With a child to nurture,
Mom had to go to work.
She soon obtained employment
As a local drugstore clerk.
Although she didn't mind it,
It wasn't quite the life
That she envisioned for herself
As mother and as wife.

Dad was in the army
As a peacetime volunteer,
But he had no intention
To make it his career.
He didn't like the army
And waited for the day
His enlistment would be over,
Still quite some time away.

When dad stopped in the drugstore
For his favorite cigarette,
He struck up a relation
With that striking young brunette.
They were often seen together
When he was home on leave,
And he wore her like insignia
Upon his khaki sleeve.

They sometimes spoke of marriage,
But found, to their dismay,
That two could never make it
On an army private's pay.

But the army's regulations
Contained the answer sought:
For a sum of money certain
A discharge could be bought.

So Momma sought assistance
From daddy's younger sister,
And outlined to her a game-plan
For freeing up her mister.
By pooling their resources
They more quickly could achieve
The necessary ransom
For her sweetheart's reprieve.

Grandpa was disapproving.
He said that Dad was wild
And much too irresponsible
To take on wife and child.
Also, he was prone to drink
And lacked maturity.
So he advised his daughter
To let the matter be.

But Momma was determined
To see the matter through,
And so began a campaign
The money to accrue.
By living very frugally,
Tightfisting every sou,
She saved up every penny
That was the army's due.

The army got the money
According to her plan.

Daddy got his discharge,
And Momma got her man.
Daddy made a bargain,
When he took Mom to wife,
And he never went back on it
Throughout their married life.

Though he oft displeased her,
Her heart did not condemn.
He never gave up drinking,
And she ne'er gave up on him.
She was always faithful.
Her faith was not betrayed,
For he belonged to Momma,
Bargained, bought and paid.

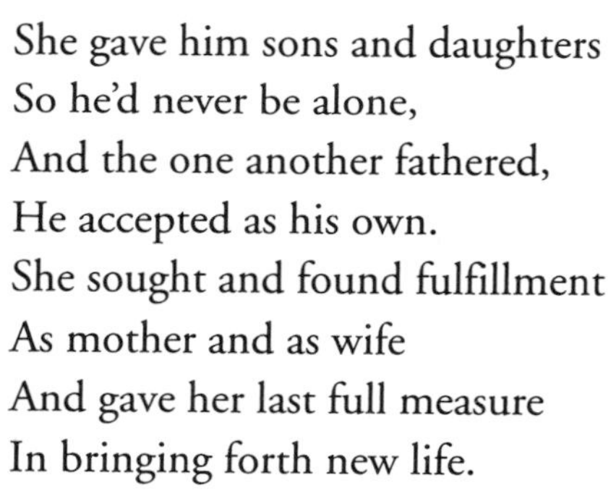

She gave him sons and daughters
So he'd never be alone,
And the one another fathered,
He accepted as his own.
She sought and found fulfillment
As mother and as wife
And gave her last full measure
In bringing forth new life.

I'm oft inclined to wonder:
Would she do it o'er again?
Did she make a wise investment
Or take it on the chin?
Anyway, I'm glad she did it,
For I have a stake, you see,
'Cause when Momma bought a husband
The deal included me.

Ours was a law-abiding family. We minded our own business, tried to do what was right and stayed out of trouble. But sometimes trouble comes looking for you.

MOM TOOK ON THE STATE POLICE

If my memory serves me well,
It was back in thirty-six
That we suffered through a spell
Of misfortunes life inflicts.

From his job Dad was laid off,
And was feeling in the dumps.
Then there was the whooping cough,
Followed closely by the mumps.

Then the cruelest cut of all,
Though it turned out quite all right,
Two state troopers paid a call
In the middle of the night.

That may not have been the worst
Of the hard times Dad was in,
Nor the last time or the first,
Mom's strong will saved his skin.

She had stood right by his side,
Though life was oft adverse,
Since she had become his bride
For the better or the worse.

But, as she never had before,
Momma pulled out all the stops
When she raised Dad's forty-four
And took aim upon those cops.

At that time in history,
I was but a little kid.
I admit I did not see
That brave deed Momma did.

So the tale that I now render,
Now that I am growing old,
Is what I still remember
Of the story often told.

In my mind it's etched so clearly
That I see it plain as day,
So I tell you most sincerely
That it happened just this way.

Sometime in the dead of night,
When shadows run so deep,
All was peaceful, calm and quiet,
And we were fast asleep.

On the door began a pounding,
To disturb and overawe,
And beyond, a voice expounding,
"Open up, this is the law."

Daddy drew the door ajar,
And in a sleep-bound stupor,
Gazed upon the shining star
Of a uniformed state trooper.

There were two, who rushed the door
And forced their way inside.
Dad's protests they would ignore;
Momma's pleas they brushed aside.

They said they were pursuing
A dangerous wanted man,
And that in the chase ensuing
Into our house he ran.

Mom knew this was a pack of lies
And to their faces stated,
But quickly came to realize,
They were inebriated.

The two began to search about,
With no apparent plan.
Their behavior left no doubt
They sought no dangerous man.

They rummaged through the cupboards,
Even in the icebox peeping,
And stripped away the covers
Where we children lay asleeping.

When Dad, who had been rather meek,
Began to make a fuss,
They said, "You are the man we seek,
Now you must come with us."

Throughout that reign of terror,
Mom had remained in bed.
A minor social error,
Which may have been misread.

When they burst in together,
Her hand, unnoticed, slid
Beneath the tick of feathers,
Where Daddy's gun was hid.

As they headed for the door,
Not expecting an attack,
She calmly raised that forty-four
And cocked the hammer back.

"My man cannot go out tonight,"
She said, "But you'll be leaving,
For if you stay within my sight,
Your widows will be grieving."

They did not fail to comprehend
The point that Mom was making,
For they were on the business end
Of her business undertaking.

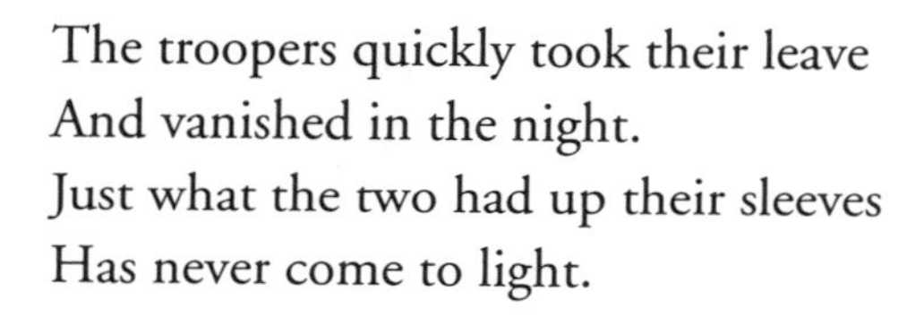

The troopers quickly took their leave
And vanished in the night.
Just what the two had up their sleeves
Has never come to light.

Once the two were out the door,
The house was locked up tight.
The kids were put to bed once more,
But Dad stayed up all night.

For several nights ensuing,
We dreamed of nothing more,
Than drunken cops pursuing
The felons to our door.

But finally, we made our peace
And, since, we've told with pride,
How Mom took on the State Police
And saved our Daddy's hide.

In the great scheme of things, one would hardly think of looking to an ordinary washtub for inspiration. In fact, if one were to give any thought at all to such an implement, it would likely be to simply regard it as an antique hardware item, once quite commonly used in hand laundering of clothing, but which has been supplanted by modern washday appliances. However, in its day, the galvanized tub was much more than a laundry device. It was at once a laundry tub, a bathtub, a food processor, and as many other things as the imagination would allow, even a source of inspiration.

THE GALVANIZED TUB

A cavernous wheel without a hub;
Zinc-clad steel of "Wheeling" prime;
Bright as a newly minted dime;
Dad's gift to Mom: a galvanized tub.

We kids regarded it a toy,
And in our play it was abused.
But soon we learned that it was used
For tasks which children don't enjoy.

Washdays saw the children going,
Pail in hand, across the track,
Carrying the river back,
Until the tub was overflowing.

Mom's companions for the day
Were the washboard and the tub.
She would plunge and soap and rub
All the dirt and grime away.

Family washday legends tell
How, with lye-steeped laundry water,
From the tub which Dad had bought her,
She would scrub the floors as well.

That homemade soap infused with lye,
On overalls or underthings,
Made colors vanish as on wings,
So, the tub was oft a vat of dye.

On Saturdays, each child in turn,
Mom would place into the tub.
From head to toe, she'd soap and scrub.
Oh, how that soap would sting and burn.

Pity Dad, poor man of clay,
Fresh from work, where coal was mined,
Black with coal dust, was consigned
To that washtub every day.

In the back yard, o'er the flame
With the garden's precious yield,
Packed in Mason jars and sealed,
A canning kettle it became.

At Halloween, when well disguised
Children on our home descended
To bob for apples some upended
In that tub and were baptized.

In the river we went swimming,
While that sturdy tub afloat,
Served as baby sister's boat,
And o'er the water she'd go skimming.

From Big Coal River's rocky floor,
Rounded lumps of coal we'd grub,
Which we placed within the tub
And floated easily to shore.

Whether Mom was cutting hair,
Busy picking corn for shucking,

Or scalding chickens for the plucking,
That faithful tub was always there.

That washtub had a great impact
Upon my life when, as a kid,
It seemed whatever that I did,
That tub always got in the act.

About that tub, do you suppose
Dad ever gave a single thought?
It was just something he had bought,
So that Mom could wash his clothes.

And as Mom labored o'er that vat,
In many ways a useful tool,
Would she regard herself a fool
To think of it as more than that?

So often ordinary things
We are inclined to take for granted,
Quite unaware that God has planted
Within our grasp a pair of wings.

For in that tub we did aspire
To cleanliness that's more than clean,
From want and poverty to glean
The strength to rise above the mire.

And like that tub, we learned that we
Are vessels fit for many uses.
Sometimes we too must know abuses,
That we may learn humility.

Should the King incline to dub
This vessel a more noble name,
None more worthy could I claim
Than Mom's old faithful "Galvanized Tub."

Just mention a treadle sewing machine and someone will surely offer the information that Grandmother or old Aunt Jane had one of those and, most likely, that it is still in the family. They are treasured items. This is the story of my mother's sewing machine. It is also about my strong-willed mother and her efforts to provide for her children during the years of the great depression.

MOMMA'S SEWING MACHINE

Momma expressed no strong ambition
For wealth or fame or social position.
She contentedly cooked and cleaned and mended
And to her family's cares attended.

But Momma had one heart's desire.
Her ambition rose no higher
Than to hope that fate somehow would bring her
A treadle sewing machine by Singer.

I count this not a selfish thought,
For clothing must be made or bought,
And children oft their clothes outgrow
Faster than the hand can sew.

But Momma realized, of course,
That she possessed no cash resource,
For every penny was always spent,
With scarcely enough to pay the rent.

How could she ever hope to glean
Enough to buy a sewing machine?
But, as philosophers would say,
In the question the answer lay.

So Momma searched the neighborhood,
Gathering up what'er she could
Of iron and brass left lying about,
And things of copper, all worn out.

Then underneath the big elm tree,
She displayed her ware for all to see
And vowed she'd get three cents a pound
When next the junkman came around.

Junkmen were numerous in that day.
Many men without jobs or pay,
With a cart or a truck and a little spunk,
Had turned to buying and selling junk.

So the junkman came, a portly gent,
And offered to pay just half a cent.
He said she couldn't do better than that,
But Momma just turned the man down flat.

He raised the ante by a half,
Which brought from Mom a scornful laugh.
But then her laugh turned to surprise.
She could scarcely believe her eyes.

For, by an amazing stroke of luck,
There upon that junkman's truck
Was the grandest sight she'd ever seen:
A Singer treadle sewing machine.

It obviously had seen much use,
With patent signs of sore abuse,
Missing parts and well worn treadle,
Flaking paint and rusted metal.

For the junk heap seemingly overdue,
But to Mom a dream come true,
That rusted relic of the machinist's art
Found its way into Momma's heart.

The haggling then got down to cases,
Determination written on their faces,
But eventually a bargain was struck
And the Singer rescued from the junkman's truck.

Everyone thought that our dear mother
Had traded one pile of junk for another.
But Momma knew, much better than we,
Just what a blessing that machine could be.

In the days that followed, she made all the stops
At junkyards and hardware and furniture shops.
Every lead and suggestion she patiently chased,
'Till each missing part had been replaced.

With infinite skill, no one knew she possessed,
The woes of that damaged machine she addressed.
She brushed and sanded the rusted metal
And carefully painted the legs and treadle.

She waxed and polished the wood veneers,
Then cleaned and oiled the movements and gears.
When she had adjusted the tension so keen,
That relic ran like a sewing machine.

With clothing of six growing children to mend,
Momma worked at her Singer for hours on end.
Sewing shirts and blouses, dresses and slacks,
Fashioning garments from designer feed sacks.

At times, when her legs became swollen and sore,
One of the children would sit on the floor,
And in response to Momma's command,
Would obediently work the treadle by hand.

That Singer did all that she asked it and more,
And repaid many-fold what it cost to restore.
Through that machine Momma's love found expression
And carried her family through the great depression.

Momma died in childbirth, of severe complications.
The children were then sent to live with relations.
Aunt Opal took the baby, just three days grown,
And, thereafter, raised little "Pete" as her own.

To live with Aunt Maude, sister Betty opted.
Young Bonnie was shortly by strangers adopted.
Dovetta was chosen by the Pridemore family,
While Grandpa kept brother Billy and me.

Aunt Zoma took home my sister Corrine,
Together with Momma's sewing machine.
Later, when I had started my own family,
She thoughtfully gave that old Singer to me.

My wife put that sewing machine to good use,
But after a while she put forth the excuse
That working the treadle was hard on her knees.
With a modern electric she could sew with all ease.

That electrical marvel lived up to its name.
The selection of stitches put the Singer to shame.
It could even embroider with two kinds of thread.
So Momma's old Singer was stored in the shed.

There it remained for a number of years,
While my children grew up and pursued their careers.
It lost all its lustre and gathered some rust.
At last I resolved to do what I must.

I passed it along to my oldest daughter,
Reminding her of all that I had taught her
About how the grandmother, whom she'd never seen,
Labored with love o'er that sewing machine.

It stands, unattended, in her living-room,
A valued antique and treasured heirloom,
Esteemed, yet rejected, now sharing no part,
Replaced by equipment that's "state of the art".

Like an unemployed workman, who's down on his luck,
Or a derelict resting on a junkman's truck,
It cries out for rescue, to service restore,
And the chance to play out another encore.

As sewing equipment, it's no longer needed,
So its plea for renewal continues unheeded.
Too old to be useful, too precious to lose,
It serves to remind, instruct and amuse.

'Twould be such a blessing, if the Giver of Grace,
With infinite power over time and space,
Would transport the Singer to that heavenly scene
Where Momma is waiting for her sewing machine.

After our mother's demise, Dad, ostensibly in an effort to keep his family together, chose to marry a woman much younger than himself. His young bride was ill-prepared to assume responsibility for so large a family, and Dad showed no signs of giving up his drinking habit, so, there was trouble from the beginning. Our new stepmother's reaction often was to go home to mother, and we kids were left to fend for ourselves, which we did rather well.

COAL SOUP

Dad was on another drunk,
His whereabouts unknown,
And Corrine, Dovetta, Billy and I
Were left at home alone
When Birdie, Dad's new teenage bride,
For one cause or another,
Took baby sister Bonnie
And went home to her mother.

Savoring our freedom,
We spent the day at play
And did some things forbidden,
But who was there to say?
Then as suppertime drew near
And hunger stalked the group,
Someone made the suggestion
That we cook a pot of soup.

Billy, who was oldest,
Was little more than eleven.
Corrine was five and I was nine,
Dovetta only seven.
We were but tender children,
Who had not learned to cook,

But having eaten lots of soup,
We knew just what it took.

Dovetta gathered vegetables
From our pantry's meager store.
I fired up the coal cookstove,
Which often was my chore.
Billy put the kettle on
And stirred in all the stuff.
Corrine insisted she could help
But wasn't big enough.

The soup began to boiling
And smelled to us just great.
We could have eaten it right then,
But Bill said we must wait.
Our stomachs growled from hunger;
Our lips could not but drool.
But suddenly the boiling stopped
As the stove began to cool.

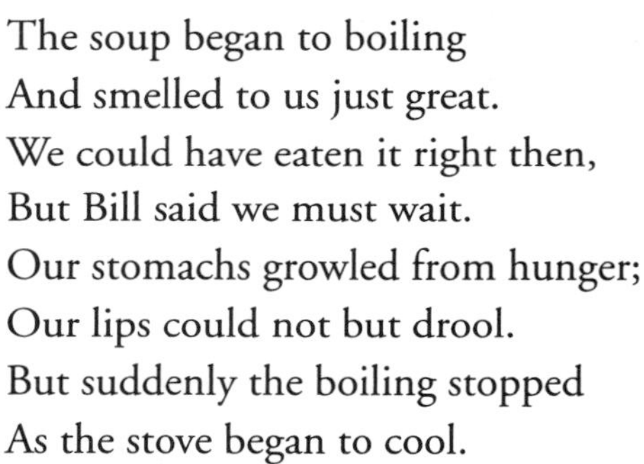

Bill set the kettle to one side
And raised the firebox lid
Then told Dovetta to add coal,
A task she sometimes did.
"Let me, Let me!" Corrine exclaimed.
Then with a sudden swoop,
She pounced upon a lump of coal
And tossed it in the soup!

Billy tried to fish it out
As, impatiently, we waited,
But in that steaming caldron
It had just disintegrated.

He stirred and searched throughout the pot
Until he realized,
The coal had mingled with the soup,
As if homogenized.

We wondered if that blackened mess,
Which was to be our feast,
Could safely be digested
By either man or beast.
We did not wish to throw it out,
For that would be a waste.
Yet none of us was brave enough
To hazard but a taste.

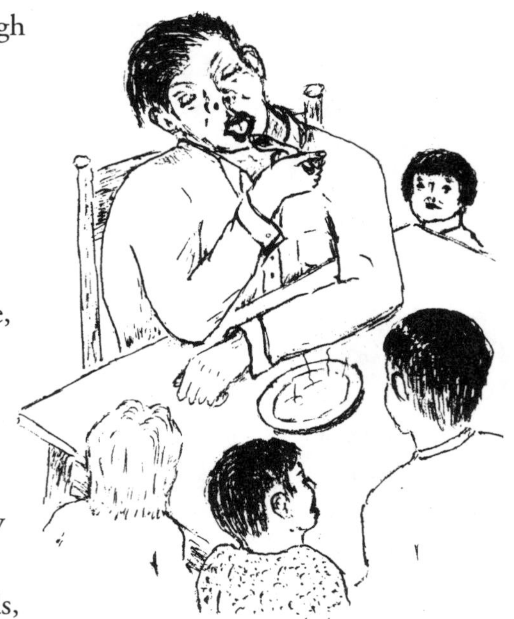

Dad, at last, arrived at home
And staggered to a seat.
He asked if we had anything
A drunken man could eat.
We quickly called a conference,
Our forces to regroup,
Then, warily, set before him
A steaming bowl of soup.

We watched him very carefully
For signs of toxicosis,
And when he asked for seconds,
We made our diagnosis.
Contaminated, though it was,
Deadly, it was not.
So we four famished children
Finished off the pot.

No doubt, you've heard the saying
And believe that it is true,

"Too many cooks will spoil the broth."
But what about too few?
I'd rather take my chances
With cooks lined pole to pole,
Than gamble on a five-year-old
With a dirty lump of coal.

I haven't lost my taste for soup.
I cook it frequently.
And friends, who once have tasted,
Ask for my recipe.
But when my brother Bill comes by
And serves him up a bowl,
He always says facetiously,
"It needs a lump of coal."

My spice rack now includes a jar
Of substance quite well known,
Marked: "Special Soup Ingredient,
For Billy's bowl alone."
When next my brother Billy
Partakes a meal with us,
I'll see he gets his favorite dish:
"Soup Bituminous."

My brother Billy was always eager to try new things and willing to take chances. I sometimes regret that I am not more like him in that respect. I have always been more conservative and thoughtful, not speaking or acting until I had considered all the possible consequences. I then usually chose the safer course, which sometimes meant taking no action at all. But as children, Billy was the dominant one, and I often found myself doing it his way, which gave me many opportunities afterward to say, "I told you so."

STREAK PREVIEW

"I dare you," my brother Bill exclaimed,
As he issued a challenge to me.
"Not me," said I, "It's much too cold,
And besides, someone might see."
But Bill was not easily dissuaded,
Once he had made up his mind,
And when adventuring, he always insisted
That his brother be not far behind.

He said he had read it somewhere
(Just where he never confessed)
That it was healthful to do some running
Each morning before you dressed.
Now, Bill took things quite literally,
And anything he saw in print
Was to him no less than Gospel,
Like a message from heaven sent.

On the other hand, I was a skeptic,
In my opinions not easy to sway,
But since Billy was older, and bigger,
He usually got his way.
With the temperature well below freezing,
He had picked this morning to propose

That we each do ten laps 'round the homestead,
Decked out in our "birthday clothes."

"Come on now, don't be a sissy,"
Bill cried as he leaped from the bed,
Taking all of the bedcovers with him,
And away to the back door he sped.
I followed with resignation,
Not sure yet just what I would do.
But when Billy peeled off his pajamas,
I reluctantly abandoned mine too.

Everyone in the house was still sleeping,
And, I hoped, in the neighborhood as well,
As Bill quickly swung the door open
And took off "like a bat out of hell."
I closed the door softly behind me,
Which, momentarily, my departure delayed,
Then I darted off after my brother
And joined in his nudist parade.

I cleared the porch like a hurdler,
My momentum gaining fast,
But as I barreled around the first corner,
I was stung by a strong arctic blast.
It sent the shivers right through me
And stopped me near dead in my track.
The tears welled up in my eyeballs.
For a moment, things seemed to go black.

I somehow avoided the rosebush
That was always grasping for me.
Then I skittered around the coal pile,
Although hardly a thing could I see.

As I made the last turn near the outhouse
And sped toward the back porch once more,
I finally caught sight of my brother,
Just as he was closing the door.

With only one lap to his credit,
He'd decided to call it a day.
Not a moment too soon to my notion,
For my strength was fast fading away.
Not a word or a glance passed between us
As we pulled on our pants and sneakers,
But we knew, for a fact, in that moment,
That we'd never make it as streakers.

While delving into my family's genealogy, I came upon this bit of interesting information.

FAMILY SECRETS

Each family has its closets
Where skeletons are hid,
Black sheep, never mentioned
Or what foul deeds they did.
Dirty linens, never washed
Or hung out on the line,
Secrets kept in darkened rooms
Where light may never shine.

I never dreamed that it was so
In my own family.
No murderers or horse thieves grew
Upon my family tree.
You can imagine my surprise,
When first the tale began,
That before she married Grandpa,
Grandma was a man!

I branded it a dirty lie,
A slander on her name,
And appealed to older relatives
To put the lie to shame.
They but confirmed what had been told
And proudly did proclaim,
"Yes, grandma really was a Mann.
That was her maiden name."

Some mornings are just too great to let go of. But they don't always start out so great. On one particular morning, I was rudely awakened by the bawling, or should I say trumpeting, of my neighbor's Hereford bull which, apparently, was being prevented by a strong barbed wire fence from doing what bulls are supposed to do. I arose just in time to see the first rays of the yet unseen sun light up the tops of the hills to the west and then creep slowly toward the valley. By the time I had dressed and had breakfast, the trumpeting had ceased and, when I stepped outside, I was treated to one of the most beautiful and tranquil scenes I have or may ever witness. I was mesmerized to the point that I could not bear to let go of that moment.

COUNTRY MORNING

How peaceful is the countryside
When darkness fades to light.
The night sounds now abated,
The world is calm and quiet
As if in meditation
At the passing of the night.

A mist upon the meadow
Surveys as darkness flees.
The dew lies heavy on the grass
And showers from the trees.
The spider's web, adorned with pearls,
Shimmers lightly in the breeze.

Emblazoned by the hidden sun,
The eastern sky bestows
A golden kiss upon the earth,
A summons from repose,
While high atop the western slope
A sunlit forest glows.

The cawing of a soaring crow
Bespeaks the newborn day
As the cautiously emerging sun
Sends forth a shining ray,
And a million sparkling diamonds gleam
Where once the dewdrops lay.

The bee begins his humming
As he flits from flower to flower.
The robin lifts a merry song
While nesting in her bower,
And I am lost in reverie
Unmindful of the hour.

Now the day has fully come,
And yet I stand and wait.
Though I'm expected elsewhere,
And already I am late,
The inertia of contentment
Makes me procrastinate.

Birds are wonderful creatures. Their bright plumage is a pleasure to behold and their seemingly happy songs can lift the saddest heart. But too much of a good thing, well, you know how the saying goes. One warm, foggy, summer night I was awakened by the loud singing of a mockingbird perched in a tree near my open bedroom window. Its concert went on for several hours, rendering sleep impossible. I tried to shoo it away, but it wouldn't budge. In desperation, I threw rocks at the tree, and it flew out, but, as soon as I had returned to my bed, it was back again, and the concert continued. Determined to make the best of the situation, I arose and penned the following plea, appropriately addressed,

TO A MOCKINGBIRD SINGING AT NIGHT

Two A.M. and still no sleep.
How long will you this vigil keep?
Concealed within your lofty bower,
Singing in the midnight hour,
Repeating sounds which you have heard,
Voiced by cricket, toad and bird,
Hour on hour, alone you sit,
Singing for the joy of it.
But on this warm and foggy night,
While all about is still and quiet,
Must you raise your voice so shrill
Close beside my windowsill?

Miles I traveled yesterday,
Scarcely stopping on the way.
My promises have all been kept,
And eagerly would I have slept,
But for this potpourri of sounds
Which in my chamber now redounds.
Enough! Enough, my feathered friend.
Of this your concert make an end.

At another time and place
Your melodies I would embrace
Or even now appreciate,
Were the hour not so late.
I applaud your artistry
And skillful use of mimicry.
Your repertoire I must admire,
But sleep is what I most desire.
So, shoo bird! Shoo! Go fly away.
Sing your songs when it is day,
Or, at the least, do this for me:
Sing in someone else's tree.

When I was a boy, living with my grandfather, it was often my task to cut the grass on the big front lawn, using an iron wheeled, reel-type push mower. It was a difficult job for a small boy and I sometimes found myself wishing that there were no grass. I now have even more grass to cut, and, even with a gasoline powered riding mower, it is a time consuming task. One day, while so engaged, and wanting to be doing other things, I blurted out that boyhood wish that there were no grass. Immediately, I was visited by this sobering thought: but what if there really were no grass? I have seen photographs, sent back to earth by space-traveling scientific probes, showing the surfaces of other planets to be devoid of all vegetation. I now see grass in a different light.

HOW DOES THE GRASS GROW?

How does the grass grow? With all haste:
Swiftly, as a race is run,
When favored by the rain and sun;
As one who has no time to waste,
Nor task to leave undone.

How does the grass grow? Hardly at all
When the earth lies baked and dry,
And no rain showers from the sky,
When autumn leaves begin to fall,
And winter's snow piles high.

How does the grass grow? Strong and tough:
Enduring winter's cold and summer's heat;
Abused by armies of trampling feet;
A carpet of leather, yet tender enough
For little lambs to eat.

How does the grass grow? Does it spin or toil
Barren wastelands to regain?

Interceding with the wind and rain,
It halts their pillage of the soil,
Earth's wounds to heal again.

How does the grass grow? With humility:
An intruder, unwanted, in another's berth;
Food for cattle its highest worth;
When clipped and groomed to uniformity,
A doormat for inhabitants of the earth.

How does the grass grow? As a caring friend:
A velvety cushion where children play;
A cool refreshing in the heat of day;
For life's weary traveler at journey's end,
A mantle o'er the clay.

How does the grass grow? By God's grace,
So, upon his name let us call,
Offering thanks for grass, green and tall,
As we contemplate other planets in space
Without any grass at all.

Sometimes the most innocent and perfectly normal childhood activity can take a wrong turn and land you in a peck of trouble. And, despite admonishment and clearly stated rules of conduct, when left alone, boys will be boys.

THE DEBUGGING

Our grandpa and our grandma
Went out to some affair,
Leaving Bill and me at home,
When no one else was there.
Grandma gave instructions
And charged us to abide,
"If your friends come out to play,
Don't let them come inside.
And don't go in the living room."
"Now Boys," our Grandpa said,
"Don't forget to wash your feet
Before you go to bed."

We played a game of croquet,
Out on the big front lawn,
Then flew our model airplanes,
'Till light was almost gone.
Then as night descended,
We both became aware
Of winking lights around us.
Fireflies were everywhere.
I caught a passing firefly.
Then Billy caught one too
And said, "I'll bet that I can catch
More lightning bugs than you!"

Bill was quite competitive.
He never let it rest.
In everything he undertook,
Bill had to be the best.
He hurried to the basement,
Returning in a snap,
With two of Grandma's canning jars,
Each with a glass-lined cap.
We rushed about the area,
Stabbing at the night,
Snatching every lightning bug
That dared to show its light.

Eventually, we realized
The game was up, no doubt.
Each time we tried to put one in,
Two or more flew out.
We never could determine
Who had the most amount.
The bugs within were, obviously,
Too numerous to count.
But Billy found that when the bugs
Began to dim their lights,
He could give the jar a shake
And switch them back to bright.

Since the hour was growing late,
We took our bugs inside
And set them on the mantel piece
Where we could view with pride.
We left the caps a bit ajar,
So they could get some air,
Then quickly washed our dirty feet
And said our bedtime prayer.

We viewed those glowworms from our bed,
And in the darkness deep,
Their lights grew ever dimmer
As we drifted off to sleep.

The next thing I remember
Was my body being shaken
As Grandpa dragged me from the bed
And urged me to awaken.
I had a revelation
That I'd done something bad,
For never, ever had I seen
My Grandpa quite so mad,
Or Grandma so beside herself,
Flailing at the air,
And telling Grandpa franticly,
"They're crawling in my hair."

Through a sleepy haze I saw
A cloud of winking stars,
But on the mantel piece, so clear,
Two empty canning jars.
Grandma's white lace curtains
And handsome crocheted rugs
Were literally teeming
With crawling lightning bugs.
I wanted to go back to bed,
But it was all for nought,
For Grandpa said, "You shall not sleep,
'Till every bug's been caught!"

It seemed a bit like *déjà vu*,
Which at one's memory tugs,
As once again we rushed about

Snatching lightning bugs.
When we our chore had finished,
We all got on our knees,
And Grandpa asked the Lord above.
"Would He, in mercy, please,
Pardon these two sinful lads
And take away their shame?"
I felt a bit uneasy
When he mentioned me by name.

At last, we were permitted
To go on back to bed,
But I was deeply troubled
By what our Grandpa said.
What we did was wrong, I guess,
And I'll take half the blame,
But why did Grandpa have to snitch
And tell the Lord my name?
Whenever Billy would recall
That night of *déjà vu*,
He always said, "Both times I caught
More lightning bugs than you."

It is generally believed that all grandparents spoil their grandchildren while expecting their parents to teach them responsibility. Not so, with our grandparents. Although less strict and less inclined to administer corporal punishment, they tried to teach and demonstrate, by example, responsible behavior. We were expected to do such normal chores as cutting the grass, carrying out the trash, feeding the chickens and collecting the eggs. Sometimes, we were even required to kill chickens and pluck their feathers and to restock the soft drink coolers at the restaurant they operated. But Grandpa went a giant step further when he assigned to Billy and me the task and responsibility of raising two pigs.

TO RAISE A PIG

Grandpa was an educator
Nine months of the year.
But when he wasn't teaching school,
He was a restaurateur.
He and Grandma had a place
They called "The Coffee Shoppe,"
Next to the theatre,
By the bus and taxi stop.

Grandpa was the manager
And tended to the till.
He handled all the money,
And paid each monthly bill.
Grandma did the cooking
And made the pies and cakes.
She baked cornbread and biscuits,
And grilled the T-bone steaks.

Delicious home-style cooking,
Served with style and grace,
Brought customers from near and far

To eat at Grandpa's place.
And early morning travelers
Would always start their day
With sausage, eggs and biscuits,
Served Grandma's special way.

Grandpa, no less than Grandma,
Was generous, indeed,
But frugal, just by nature,
"Waste not, want not," his creed.
So it disturbed his conscience
And filled him with dismay
To see so much uneaten food
They had to throw away.

I heard him telling Grandma
That he had found a way
To put to use the wasted food
They threw out every day.
His plan would soon eliminate
Much of the food debris
And teach two boys the meaning of
Responsibility.

So Grandpa went to market,
With brother Bill in tow,
And carried back two burlap sacks
That writhed and wriggled so.
From each bag came a squealing pig,
And one made straight for me.
Instantly, I knew its name:
Responsibility.

Grandpa said those piglets
Were ours to feed and tend,

Ours to slop and water,
To keep securely penned,
To ply with fresh cut hogweeds
And furnish lots of swill,
'Till they were full-grown porkers,
Fatted for the kill.

He said it was a business deal,
A sort of partnership.
He had bought the piglets
And would the pen equip.
He'd provide the food scraps
And would our mentor be.
But for our part, we must assume
Responsibility.

I waited for the bottom line,
But hadn't heard it yet,
So, I asked, "From this partnership,
What do we stand to get?"
Grandpa explained, "We'll sell the hogs
When prices are the best.
I'll take my expenses
And yours shall be the rest."

Grandpa chose the building site,
Where none should take offense.
The owner gave permission
And got his recompense.
A suitable location,
It was, without denial,
But far from Grandpa's restaurant,
About a quarter-mile.

With lumber from the sawmill,
We built a sturdy shed
And made a v-shaped hog trough
Where piglets could be fed.
We raised a tight enclosure,
Three to four feet high,
And when we poured in water,
Those piglets had a sty.

Grandpa paid a man to come
And on them "operate."
He deemed it necessary
For pigs to put on weight.
First, he neutered Billy's pig,
And then, he cut on mine.
I still remember to this day
That smell of turpentine.

Throughout the days to follow
We filled those porkers needs:
Water by the barrel,
Armloads of hogweeds,
Food waste from the restaurant,
Mixed to make a swill,
Which bucketful by bucketful
We carried up the hill.

At first, when they were piglets,
It wasn't such a chore.
But as they grew much larger,
They ate a whole lot more.
The buckets too were bigger
And heavier the weight.
So I devised a two-wheeled cart
To carry all that freight.

Those pigs enjoyed a life of ease,
While I'd become their slave.
I was a bit resentful,
But to the task I clave.
For I found comfort in the thought,
That I would be set free,
Once I had acquired
Responsibility.

Sometimes in the evening,
Once the pigs were fed,
I'd lay aside my buckets
And climb atop the shed.
In the hush of twilight,
Between the sty and sky,
I'd dream of instant riches
And of the things I'd buy.

Finally, the day arrived.
The pigs, just eight months old,
Were fully grown and fattened
And ready to be sold.
The selling price of hogs was up,
But lest they downward dash,
We took those hogs to market
And turned them into cash.

Billy's hog brought forty-nine,
Mine just forty-four.
I don't know why the difference.
His pig, I guess, ate more.
Grandpa took out expenses.
The remainder, I suppose,
Went to Hicks' Department Store
To pay for our new clothes.

Grandpa bought us each new shoes,
A two-piece Sunday suit,
A white, stiff-collared, long-sleeved shirt
And bright bow tie, to boot.
At church, Grandpa was very proud
To see us dressed so neat,
'Till I took off my new suit coat
And laid it on the seat.

Grandpa's conservation plan
Had served him very well.
Were two lads more responsible?
He really couldn't tell.
But since we turned a profit,
Which merited his praise,
Next year he planned to buy more pigs
For Bill and me to raise.

I never saw the money,
I thought that I had earned.
I didn't get my freedom,
But this, perhaps, I learned:
To keep your suit-coat on in church,
Apparently, must be
The absolute quintessence of
Responsibility.

I have described Mud River as a quiet, friendly, boy-size river. And it is, most of the time. However, as I have suggested on several occasions, it has another nature. It can show anger. In fact, at times, it seems to be downright mean. Now, I don't blame the river for its sudden and destructive mood changes, because they are the result of circumstances beyond its control. Just as some people I know get grumpy and irritable during foul weather and take their frustrations out on innocent parties, Mud River also reacts, sometimes angrily, to changes in the weather. How would you like it if someone dumped on you a bigger load than a person of your size and ability could reasonably be expected to manage? Well, when that happens to Mud River, it gets so mad that it climbs right out of its banks. And then, watch out!

MUD RIVER RISING

The rain continued falling
All day and through the night,
Yet, showed no signs of slacking
At dawning's gloomy light.
It beat upon the windows
And fell to earth in sheets,
Raising spatters ankle high
Upon the blacktop street.

The roadside drainage ditches
Were running at their fill
And spilled out on the pavement
At the bottom of the hill.
The creeks in every hollow
Had grown to double-size.
And folks in town were cautioned:
"Mud River's on the rise."

From the tiny attic window,
Of the dormer where we slept,

We watched the rising river
As swiftly by it swept.
Bill fussed about the weather
Which, in the spoiler's role,
Had blocked the summer sunshine
And closed the "swimmin' hole."

Mud River, only yesterday,
A quiet, lazy "crick,"
Had become a raging torrent,
Coursing brown and thick,
And tossing on its billows,
As though in righteous wrath,
The flotsam of man's refuse
Abandoned in its path.

Over in the Sweetland Store,
Some Townsfolk were attuned
To fears that flooded highways
Would leave the town marooned.
But in the lower part of town,
Close by the river Mud,
Most folks were bent on saving
Their belongings from the flood.

"Jack and Jimmie, Get the pigs
On up to higher ground
For if they're left there in the pen,
Most likely they will drown.
Elevate the furniture.
Leave nothing on the floor.
Hurry! Don't forget the cat.
Mud River's at the door!"

As usual, first, at Jesse's place,
Mud River left its banks
And spread out in a battle line,
As soldiers formed in ranks.
Then, like a mighty army,
Moved by the trumpet's sound,
It swept across the pavement
And occupied the town.

At first, a moving yellow stain,
But soon, a holocaust,
As the raging Mud reclaimed
Its ancient floodplain lost.
It sowed in all the houses
Ruin and despair.
The Mud has no compassion
When it goes on a tear.

The covered bridge no longer
Spanned the river Mud,
Its massive stone abutments
Surrounded by the flood.
Downstream, the cable swinging bridge,
Suspended from a tree
Was dragging on the rushing tide
And gathering debris.

We watched in rapt excitement
From windows high and dry.
But Bill was discontented.
His plans had gone awry.
As darkness swiftly gathered,
With yet no end in sight,
Bill got the crazy notion
To swim the flood at night.

I said that was the dumbest,
And endeavored to dissuade.
But Bill conned cousin Jimmie,
And soon a plan was laid.
I remained in opposition,
But well did Billy know,
That if they two went swimming,
Then I would also go.

We stripped down to our trousers.
To fate I was resigned.
No one would note our absence.
The flood was on their minds.
We planned to go up river,
Jump in, then with the flow,
Swim down to Sweetland's landing
Or somewhere on below.

The rain was lightly falling,
And darkness ruled the land,
As we trudged up the hardroad
Searching for the strand.
The waters covered everything.
The road we could not see.
The Mud was lost in darkness,
And so, thought I, were we.

Bill probed the murky waters.
We joined in his pursuits
And came upon the river bank
At a place known as "The Roots."
The Mud was dark as coal tar,
Rough as a wind-swept lake,
Swift as a winter streaker
And meaner than a snake!

Bill raised up on the tree root,
Released a chilling scream,
Then plunged into the river
And vanished in the stream.
Jim dove in behind him,
Cutting the wave like a knife,
Leaving me there in darkness,
Hanging on for life.

I mustered all my courage
And eased into the stream.
The shadows closed around me.
I was in a horrid dream.
Floating debris flowed o'er me.
Demons were lurking below,
Dragging me down to the bottom.
I was caught in the undertow.

I struggled to keep my head up.
My arms were weak as clay.
Panic spawned confusion.
I sensed I was slipping away.
My short life passed before me.
I could see it end in the flood.
Then Billy grabbed my elbow
And pulled me from the Mud.

Returning from the river,
Humbled, but yet proud,
We saw on the porch at Grandpa's,
A small, but growing, crowd.
Their presence in the darkness,
Long past the eventide,
Put in mind the notion
That someone there had died.

We entered through the basement,
Completing our short round-trip,
And washed in the wooden barrel
That caught the faucet's drip,
Then hurried to the attic
To change our soggy clothes.
Just how we went unnoticed
Is anyone's suppose.

Grandpa's porch was weary,
But bravely bore the weight
Of townsfolk gathered on it,
Their woes to contemplate.
They thanked the God in Heaven
That Grace did so abound,
To lift them from the waters
To blessed "higher ground."

"Swing the front door open.
You're welcome, one and all.
Move the furniture aside.
Lay beds from wall to wall.
Grandpa's house is haven
For every lad and lass
Who needs a place of refuge
'Till storm and flood shall pass."

"The men will take the living room.
The ladies will repair
To bedrooms on the second floor
And with the young girls share.
Babes in arms with mothers
Shall sleep in their embrace.
The boys will bunk together
And share the attic space."

The rain upon the metal roof
Hums a lullaby.
Gentle winds disperse the clouds
And slowly clear the sky.
The sounds of conversation fade,
'Till heard is not a peep,
As refugees in Grandpa's house
Drift silently to sleep.

The smell of brewing coffee
Bespeaks another day.
Grandma's making biscuits,
And gravy's on the way.
With scrambled eggs and bacon,
Who could remain abed?
But Grandma says, "Be patient boys,
'Till others have been fed."

The men are first at breakfast,
For they have work to do;
Then, mothers and young infants
And grandma's "breakfast crew;"
Next, silly girls, who "table talk"
And do things just for "show,"
And constantly remind the boys,
"Ladies first, you know."

When the boys, the last in line,
Receive the breakfast call
And sit down at the table,
Eleven boys in all,
There's bacon, ham and sausage,
Gravy, eggs and bread.
And Grandma keeps it coming,
'Till everyone is fed.

Grandma's favorite baking pan
Held just an even dozen.
"Who got the extra biscuit?"
That got the table buzzin'.
When breakfast time had ended,
We learned that biscuit's fate
When Gene, my red head nemesis,
"Found" it 'neath his plate.

With breakfast feeding over,
We take a look around
To see the flood-caused damage
In the lower part of town.
The waters have receded,
But all about we see
A coat of sticky yellow mud
And tons of wet debris.

Days will pass before some folk
Reclaim their habitat,
But others, better off, will soon
Lay out the welcome mat.
They all receive assurance,
That should the need arise,
At Grandpa's house they'll always find
A place to close their eyes.

Townsfolk would not soon forget
When rains came pouring down
And sent Mud River o'er its banks
To terrorize the town.
And three young lads would always keep
The memory in flower,
Of the time they "rode the tiger"
In Mud River's darkest hour.

Every young lad dreams of sailing off to some foreign shore, fending off an attack by cut-throat pirates or leading a squadron of fighting ships into battle. Mud River is far from the nearest ocean but, for a moment, one hot dog-day afternoon, we lived out the dream.

THE GREAT MUD RIVER NAVAL ENGAGEMENT

The Sweetland store had folded,
Its doors forever closed.
A going-out-of-business sale
Its merchandise disposed.
The wrecking crew had labored,
'Till where the store had been,
Remained but splintered timbers
And a pile of roofing tin.

That debris-strewn lot became
Our favorite place to play.
But that pile of rusting metal
Was always in the way.
As oft the wind would scatter it,
We piled it up anew.
Then Billy got the notion
To make a tin canoe.

From a single sheet of metal
A hull was crudely formed.
The sides, with staves and wire,
Were strengthened and conformed.
The bow was crimped and folded.
The edges fast impaled.
The stern was just a wooden plank
To which the sides were nailed.

With streams of melted coal tar
Each seam was joined and sealed
And every nail-hole covered
With daubs of tar congealed.
At last, when all was finished,
That vessel, trim and staunch,
Was dragged down to Mud River
And readied for the launch.

We found it quite unstable,
Rather flail from stem to stern,
Inclined to take on water
And quick to overturn.
But with a bit of practice,
We learned to compensate
And, with bucket lids for paddles,
Began to navigate.

The prototype was Billy's.
The second one was mine.
Then more and more such craft came off
Our crude assembly line.
One for Bobby, one for Gene,
For Jack and Jimmie too,
'Till each boy in our neighborhood
Had his own tin canoe.

At once, that solved the problem
Of that pile of rusting tin.
But, as well as I remember,
We played not there again.
For the scene of action shifted
To that muddy little stream,
As hearts became inspired
To live the sailor's dream.

We cruised the waters of the Mud
Up to the "swimmin' hole"
Then downstream to the covered bridge,
With neither plan nor goal.
At times we paddled leisurely.
Sometimes it was a race
From Sweetland's rocky landing
To Jesse Adkins' place.

We looked upon our vessels
As gallant "men-of-war,"
Sailing on the briny,
Off to some foreign shore.
Bob and I were cruisers.
"Destroyer" suited Gene.
Bill and Jack were battleships
And Jim, a submarine.

Folks along the river
Would from their houses pour
To watch that great flotilla
Sweep past from shore to shore.
Old Louis Sweetland, dead and gone,
Would rise up in his grave
If he but knew his leaky roof
Was cruising on the wave.

Then came the curse of "dog days,"
Which gentle ways repeal:
Those sticky days of summer
When sores refuse to heal;
When food is prone to spoilage
And dogs are known to bite;
When tempers rise with temperature
And young boys quarrel and fight.

No one can right remember
Who flung the gauntlet down,
Or where the line was drawn or crossed,
Nor may the truth be found.
But in a heated moment
Somehow the line was crossed,
And on that steamy afternoon
The fragile peace was lost.

How quickly sides were chosen
And forces brought to bear.
"Dog-dares" and ultimatums
Hung in that heavy air.
Two strong roof-tin armadas
Were drawn up in array.
The battle flags were hoisted
And we sailed into the fray.

Gene, the dread destroyer,
Was first on the attack.
He had a score to settle
That went a long way back.
He rammed me with a glancing blow
That really "rocked the boat."
My cruiser took on water,
But somehow stayed afloat.

Bill's heavy battle wagon
Steamed in pursuit of Jack,
Who managed to elude him
Then went on the attack.
He connected with a broadside
That ended Bobby's plans.
His cruiser turned upon its side
And went down with all hands.

Gene circled back to finish me,
But promptly was engaged
By Jim's marauding submarine
And, as the battle raged,
I bailed my flooded bilges
Into that muddy stream
And, finally, was able
To get up a head of steam.

Jimmy was no match for Gene
And tried to give the slip.
But with his after-deck awash,
He cried, "abandon ship."
At my command, "Full steam ahead,"
I set a course for Gene
As he bestowed the *coup de grace*
On Jimmie's submarine.

Bill finally caught up with Jack
And, as those titans clashed,
Bill's prow was lifted skyward
And down on Jack it crashed.
Bill slowly settled by the stern.
Jack went down like a stone.
Then only Gene and I remained
To fight the war alone.

I rammed him hard amidships.
Destruction was complete.
Surprise was etched upon his face
And, ah, revenge was sweet.
Yet, when I saw him sinking,
I reached a hand to save
But Gene, still "the destroyer,"
Dragged me beneath the wave.

A calm swept over the waters
Where late the battle raged.
The beast that ruled the afternoon
Had finally been caged.
No murmur of the vanquished,
Nor cry of victory,
Was heard or found expression
In all that silent sea.

The survivors gathered on the shore
And counted up the cost.
What casualties we suffered
In that fearsome holocaust!
No arm of flesh was broken,
Nor shed one drop of blood,
But the great Mud River Navy
Lay buried in the mud.

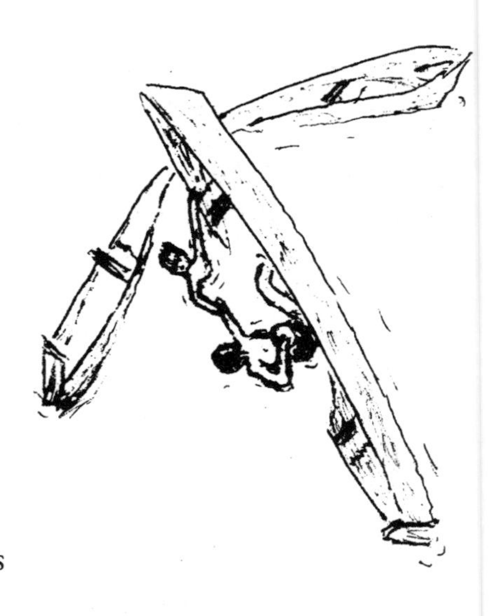

I have heard that at Trafalgar
Nelson crushed the Spanish fleet,
That the U.S. Navy whipped the Japs
Whenever they would meet,
That the British sent the Bismarck
To the bottom with a thud,
But was ever there a conflict
Like the battle of the Mud?

Once the war dust settled
And dog-day madness passed,
Boyhood friendships flourished
And through the years would last.
We oft and long debated
Which side had lost or won,
But, in this we found agreement,
Oh boy, did we have fun!

More than fifty years after the event described in "The Rescue," my brother, Bill, who had recently lost his wife to illness, discovered the identity of the young lady whom he had saved from drowning in Mud River. He learned that she too had recently lost her marriage mate. Bill called on her and the two began dating. They shared a love for dancing and were frequently the first couple on the floor when the band began to play. Romance blossomed, but alas, it was not to be, for Bill soon contracted an incurable illness that quickly robbed him of his physical abilities. He could no longer dance with his beloved Avinell, but he often dreamed that he was again in her embrace, moving about the dance floor, as the band played their favorite tune. Following are the lyrics to a song, composed especially for Bill and Avinell, which expresses Bill's affection for Avinell, his hopes for a deeper relationship with her and, ultimately, his recognition of the hopelessness of the situation. It is included in the ***Mud River Tales*** as a fitting, albeit tragic, sequel to "The Rescue."

AVINELL'S WALTZ

How I love to dance with Avinell
In a rendezvous we know so well.
When she hears the band, she's reaching for my hand.
We're in a wonderland where lovers dwell.
When I gaze into her lovely face
And feel the gentle touch of her embrace,
Anyone could see that she's in love with me,
And I'm in love with Avinell.

Counting all the charms of Avinell,
Captured by the magic of her spell,
Praying that the dance will lead into romance
And that a touch, perchance, alone will tell
That my heart is waiting for a sign,
And longs to hear her say that she'll be mine.
If she only will, I'll always be her Bill,
And she will be my Avinell.

Fading now, the moon withdraws its beam.
Stars that brightly shown no longer gleam.
Swiftly comes the day. We've danced the night away.
The band begins to play a parting theme.
In the eyes of Avinell I see
Reflections of a love that cannot be.
Morning gilds the skies. I wake and realize
That Avinell is but a dream.

In the sleepy Town of Hamlin and along Mud River, life moved at a leisurely pace. No one ever seemed to be in a hurry, unless the river was about to come pouring over its banks. Yet, there never seemed to be enough hours in the day to accomplish all the things we set out to do. So, we stretched out the day, as much as possible, by taking full advantage of that brief period known as twilight. It was sort of a winding-down time when we could enjoy a beautiful sunset, catch lightning bugs in a jar or sit and listen to Jesse play his fiddle. Twilight is, indeed, a most pleasant way to end the day and a most appropriate way to bring these ***Mud River Tales*** to a conclusion.

MUD RIVER TWILIGHT

The birds which sang at daybreak
Have flown away to nest.
The blazing sun of noonday
Now settles in the west,
Casting lengthened shadows,
Which creep across the grass,
And a panoply of colors
Beyond the prismed glass.

Milk cows at the drawbars,
Chewing on the cud,
Await the evening milking.
It's twilight on the Mud.
Fading rays of sunset
Ascend the court house dome.
And on the breeze a whistle
Entreats, "Come home! Come home!"

The crimson sky, reluctantly,
Gives way to shades of night.
And in the darkened heavens
A billion stars ignite.

As moonlight filters through the trees
Atop the eastern hill,
There comes to ear the haunting sound
Of a lonely whippoorwill.

Now, fresh upon the air is heard
A familiar fiddle tune,
As Jesse mounts his front porch stage
And serenades the moon.
Night tolls my leave to linger
And sends me on my way
As twilight on Mud River
Concludes another day.

EPILOGUE

As I think back on my childhood and recall all the negative factors which, today, many authorities regard as influential in shaping our lives, I cannot but wonder why my siblings and I did not wind up in prison or rehabilitation centers or worse. We were poor; so poor that we had to move almost as often as the rent came due. The most important consequence of this nomadic lifestyle was that we had to change schools frequently, which played havoc with our education. A possible positive factor in this, based on the adage that "what you don't know won't hurt you," is the fact that we did not know we were poor. We wore hand-me-down clothing, were glad to have it and did not expect more. Our meals, at times, consisted of cornbread and cornmeal gravy for breakfast, cornmeal mush for lunch and fried mush for supper, often served with wild greens, picked along the railroad track. My father was, or was working on becoming, an alcoholic, which created turmoil in the family and affected his ability to remain employed at a time when jobs were quite scarce. Our mother died unexpectedly, causing a breakup of the family as a unit and dispersal of the children among relatives. My father's subsequent remarriage reunited the family, but introduced a stepmother who was little more than a child herself and totally unprepared for the responsibilities of motherhood. Over a period of time, she reduced her responsibilities by causing some of her charges to be placed again in the care of relatives and by persuading our father to allow one of his children to be adopted by strangers. The others left home as soon as they were able to provide for themselves. The one stabilizing factor, during this rather tumultuous period, was the unceasing concern, loving care and influence of our grandparents, both paternal and maternal.

Despite this impressive array of depressingly negative features of our childhood, I am pleased to report that we survived to adulthood, went on to become responsible citizens, married other responsible citizens and raised children whose lives, I think, are richer because of our experiences. None of us became rocket scientists or nuclear physicists. Three of us served honorably in the U. S. Air Force, and two made a career of it. One married an Air Force officer and another a college professor. All of us graduated from high school. Three attended college, two of whom graduated, and one completed law school, becoming a lawyer and a judge. Our mother would be pleased and, perhaps, surprised to see what her sons and daughters have become. Our grandfather would be pleased and proud, but I don't think he would be at all surprised.

The time I spent in my grandfathers's house, in Hamlin and upon Mud River, was the happiest time of my life. Of course, there were unpleasant occasions, such as the death of my grandfather and moving out of his house, but, all in all, it was a good time to be alive. Billy and I were allowed a great deal of freedom. We had the run of the town and the nearby countryside, including the river, and could do pretty much as we pleased so long as we didn't get into trouble and were home by dark. I'm sure that we did some things which displeased our grandfather, but we held him in such high regard that we were determined to do nothing to dishonor him. He did not consider it necessary to come and check on us, nor did he quiz us as to where we had been or what we had been doing. However, if he assigned us a task to perform and found it undone, he was quick to reprimand. I have always believed that folks in town kept an eye on us on his behalf. Not that they were his spies or tale bearers, but, because he was their friend, they considered it their responsibility to see that we lived up to his expectations. I can recall many occasions when one of the townsfolk would say to us, "Boys, I don't think your grandfather would approve of what you are doing." That was enough. And it is still enough. I find that when I am about to embark upon a course of action which entails some moral or ethical hair-splitting, I hear, in the distant reaches of my mind, a familiar voice questioning, "Boy, would your grandfather approve of what you are doing?"

The world has taken a lot of turns since the days when we leisurely plied the waters of Mud River in our roof tin canoes. Technological advances have transformed the way people live. We have modern appliances and machinery, which make our work easier. Cellular phones and e-mail give us the ability to communicate, instantly, with anyone, anywhere in the world except, perhaps, our treating physician. Through television, we are, instantly, aware of every natural or man-made disaster, and every real or perceived threat to our existence. Life may be easier, but it is often overwhelming. We long for a time when life moved at a more leisurely pace and problems, if not fewer, were, at least, more manageable. Would we return to that time, if we could? Probably not. Still, wouldn't it be nice if, occasionally, we could just open a door to that era, ever so slightly, slip in and spend a few moments? Whenever that thought overtakes you, take the phone off the hook, turn off the television, find a comfortable chair, and revisit the ***Mud River Tales***.